THE GUARDS
CAME THROUGH

An Illustrated History of the Guards in the Great War

THE GUARDS
CAME THROUGH

An Illustrated History of the Guards in the Great War

SIMON DOUGHTY

Third Millennium
Publishing

Above: *2nd Grenadiers 'The Bermondsey B'hoys' inside Wellington Barracks, 1914 or 1915.*

First published in Great Britain in 2016 by
Third Millennium Publishing, an imprint of Profile Books Ltd

3 Holford Yard
Bevin Way
London WC1X 9HD
United Kingdom
www.tmiltd.com

A CIP catalogue record for this book is available from the British Library.

ISBN: 978 1 908990 57 0
Design: Susan Pugsley and Matthew Wilson
Editorial project manager: Hannah Bowen
Proofreading: Peter Salmon
Indexing: Neil Curtis

Reprographics by Studio Fasoli, Italy
Printed and bound by Printer Trento srl
on acid-free paper from sustainable forestry

CONTENTS

There is some curious magic that can transform a group of individuals into something much greater than the sum of its individual members. Individuals can be astonishingly brave on their own, but, as members of a like-minded group of comrades, they become capable of even greater acts of bravery and self-sacrifice.

There can be no doubt that The Guards discovered the secret of creating that group-inspired morale a long time ago. The history of The Guards from their earliest days is full of stories of individual acts of exceptional bravery and self-sacrifice. It should therefore come as no surprise to find such remarkable stories of group and individual acts of supreme courage which they performed during what was one of the most brutal wars in human history.

'The Guards Came Through' reveals the power of that magic, and shows just how the display of 'corporate morale' can influence and encourage others when things are going really badly.

INTRODUCTION

Professor Sir Michael Howard, OM, CH, CBE, MC, FBA

This history of the Brigade of Guards during the First World War is in many ways a microcosm of that of the entire British Army on the Western Front. It begins with the mobilisation of the regular units for a conflict that was expected to last for at the most a very few months. Their members were all professionals who had learned their trade the hard way in South Africa a decade earlier: expert marksmen, cavalry trained to reconnoitre and to fight on foot as well as mounted; artillery working in close support of their infantry even if still disdainful of indirect fire – an army as good and perhaps better than any in Europe even if, as the Kaiser is reported to have remarked, contemptibly small. They would acquit themselves respectably in the first bewildering encounter battles on the Belgian frontier before being forced into a long and punishing retreat that tested their discipline and endurance to the limit. They were flung into the First Battle of Ypres – their last experience of the kind of war for which they had been trained. There the old army stood, fought, and, all too many of them, died.

Their survivors then had to learn, in the ditches they hastily scrabbled in the sodden fields of Flanders, the sombre arts of trench warfare. They launched their first offensives – sadly unsuccessful – at Neuve Chapelle and Festubert. They were to suffer terribly from the incompetence of the High Command at Loos. Then began the long and bloody learning curve that, through the Somme, Passchendaele and the near disaster of the German offensive of March 1918, would gradually forge what remained of that 'contemptibly small' army into a force numbered in millions, expert in all the complexities of industrial warfare, that would play a leading role in the victorious campaign of 1918.

In this army the Brigade of Guards was from the very beginning to play a central part, but from the start it maintained its unmistakable identity. That it was able to do so was due largely to the fact that very early on in the war its units were amalgamated into a single Guards Division which imposed its unique characteristics on every man who served in it. As Simon Doughty explains in this excellent study, 'Guardsmen commanded Guardsmen; the staffs were Guardsmen; and the supporting arms, such as the Artillery, Engineers and Service Corps, became part of this cohesive grouping where excellence, attention to detail, and never accepting anything but the best was part of an ingrained culture and *esprit de corps*'. So from the moment they joined up, recruits found themselves in a world where (in the words of Harold

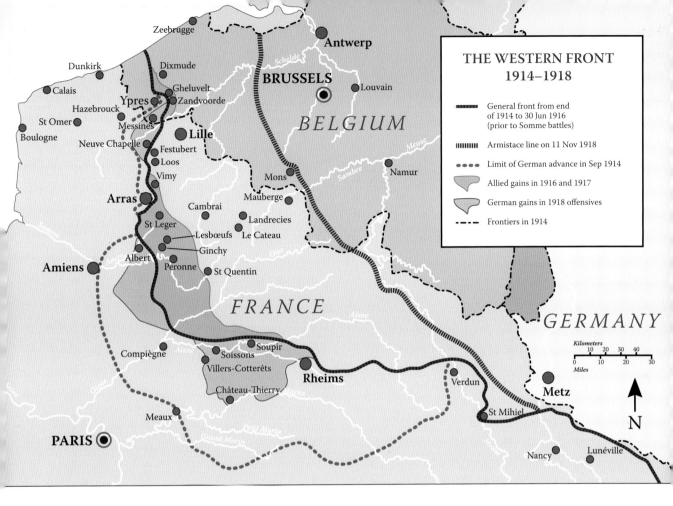

Macmillan, who served in it with exemplary gallantry), 'If anything was done, it must be done as well as possible' and that gave him, as it has given all who have shared that experience, 'a view of perfection which I didn't have before'. It was a standard that would remain unaltered through five gruelling years.

But this was not just a military unit forged by drill sergeants. It was, and remains, *a family*. Over and over again I found in these pages names that I knew so well from the history that I was privileged to write of the Coldstream Guards in the Second World War – their fathers, perhaps, or their uncles. The same names are still on regimental lists now and would have been there two centuries ago. But all too many of those in these pages are of boys killed before they could have any children of their own; killed doing what they had been brought up to do even before they joined their regiment: leading from the front.

So this book is not just the history of a military unit; it is a family memorial worthy to complement those five Guardsmen who today stand so proudly on guard on Horse Guards Parade. It is a family perhaps best described, warts and all, by a young man who briefly joined it and perhaps found there a happiness denied him in his sad later life – Prince of Wales, later Duke of Windsor:

> The Guards Division was a great club, and if tinged with snobbishness it was the snobbishness of tradition, discipline, perfection and sacrifice. They were the shock troops of the British Army; their prestige was purchased in blood.

AUTHOR PREFACE

This book is about the Household Cavalry and Brigade of Guards during the Great War. They set standards of excellence to which other regiments aspired, an invaluable contribution to a much larger effort from across Great Britain and the Empire.

The history of a single regiment in a war is a long one, while this book tells the story of seven regiments in comparatively few pages. For this reason it has not been possible to follow every action and heroic deed, but hopefully the stories covered here are indicative of others, some that are known and recorded elsewhere, while others are sadly not.

The size and roles of these regiments, listed on page 12, changed due to the impact of casualties and the need to adapt to the demands of trench warfare. The 1st (Royal) Dragoons, the senior cavalry regiment of the line, was not a Guards regiment during the war, but did amalgamate many years later with The Royal Horse Guards, and so is mentioned in this book. The full titles of each regiment have been shortened here, particularly where the actions of several are described together (for example, 1st Battalion Grenadier Guards has become 1st Grenadiers, etc.). The modern spelling of Sergeant is used throughout, although it was Serjeant during the Great War and remained so until the early 1950s. The rank of Guardsman was not formally adopted until after the war as the King's gift, although it was used before then, as it is now, to describe those soldiers of all ranks who have the privilege to serve in one of the Guards regiments.

I would like to thank Major General Edward Smyth-Osbourne and his staff at Headquarters Household Division, Julian Platt, Founder of Third Millennium, and Dr Neil Titman, formerly Publishing Director, for their support throughout this project. I would also like to thank the many people who have encouraged and helped me during the writing of this book. Any errors and omissions that remain are mine alone.

During the Great War, 14,870 soldiers of the Guards regiments were killed and over 50,000 were wounded, some dying later of their injuries. The lives of those who survived were irrevocably changed by the war, and some of them bore deep scars for the remainder of their lives. We owe them an incalculable debt of gratitude, and it is to these Guardsmen, and to those who were attached to Guards regiments during the war, that this book is dedicated. Winston Churchill, who admired the 'System of the Guards' enormously, wrote this as a tribute to all those who lost their lives:

> Unconquerable except by death, which they had conquered, they have set up a monument of native virtue which will command the wonder, the reverence and the gratitude of our island people as long as we endure as a nation among men.

Simon Doughty
London
May 2016

'The Guards Came Through'

SIR ARTHUR CONAN DOYLE; PUBLISHED IN THE TIMES, *23 JUNE 1917*

Men of the 21st
Up by the Chalk Pit Wood,
Weak with our wounds and our thirst,
Wanting our sleep and our food,
After a day and a night—
God, shall we ever forget!
Beaten and broke in the fight,
But sticking it—sticking it yet.
Trying to hold the line,
Fainting and spent and done,
Always the thud and the whine,
Always the yell of the Hun!
Northumberland, Lancaster, York,
Durham and Somerset,
Fighting alone, worn to the bone,
But sticking it—sticking it yet.

Never a message of hope!
Never a word of cheer!
Fronting Hill 70's shell-swept slope,
With the dull, dead plain in our rear.
Always the whine of the shell,
Always the roar of its burst,
Always the tortures of hell,
As waiting and wincing we cursed
Our luck and the guns and the Boche,
When the Corporal shouted "Stand to!"
And I heard some one cry, "Clear the front for the Guards!"
And the Guards came through.

Our throats they were parched and hot,
But Lord, if you'd heard the cheers!

Irish and Welsh and Scot,
Coldstream and Grenadiers.
Two brigades, if you please,
Dressing as straight as a hem,
We—we were down on our knees,
Praying for us and for them!
Praying with tear-wet cheek,
Praying with outstretched hand,
Lord, I could speak for a week,
But how could you understand!
How should your cheeks be wet,
Such feelin's don't come to you.
But when can me or my mates forget,
When the Guards came through!

"Five yards left extend!"
It passed from rank to rank.
Line after line with never a bend,
And a touch of the London swank.
A trifle of swank and dash,
Cool as a home parade,
Twinkle and glitter and flash,
Flinching never a shade,
With the shrapnel right in their face
Doing their Hyde Park stunt,
Keeping their swing at an easy pace,
Arms at the trail, eyes front!
Man, it was great to see!
Man, it was fine to do!
It's a cot and a hospital ward for me,
But I'll tell 'em in Blighty, wherever I be,
How the Guards came through.

The Guards Regiments

Household Cavalry

Household Cavalry Composite Regiment

1st Life Guards

2nd Life Guards

Royal Horse Guards, amalgamated in 1969 with

1st (Royal) Dragoons

Foot Guards

1st Battalion Grenadier Guards

2nd Battalion Grenadier Guards

3rd Battalion Grenadier Guards

4th Battalion Grenadier Guards

1st Battalion Coldstream Guards

2nd Battalion Coldstream Guards

3rd Battalion Coldstream Guards

4th Battalion Coldstream Guards (Pioneers)

1st Battalion Scots Guards

2nd Battalion Scots Guards

1st Battalion Irish Guards

2nd Battalion Irish Guards

1st Battalion Welsh Guards

Special Units – Formed During the Great War

The Household Battalion (1916–1918)

The Guards Machine Gun Regiment (1918–1920)

    1st Battalion (1st Life Guards)

    2nd Battalion (2nd Life Guards)

    3rd Battalion (Royal Horse Guards)

    4th Battalion (Foot Guards)

The Guards Entrenching (later Works) Battalion (1915–1918)

The Household Brigade Officer Cadet Battalion (1917–1919)

The Household Cavalry, each of the five Foot Guard regiments, and the Guards Machine Gun Regiment had a reserve battalion in England, to take men who were left behind because they were under age or unfit for war service, or reservists who were surplus to immediate requirements. Recruits passed through these reserve units after their basic training, as did the sick and wounded.

The Guards Division badge, the 'all-seeing eye', adopted during the Great War.

ACKNOWLEDGEMENTS

I would like to thank Major General Edward Smyth-Osbourne and all at HQ Household Division for giving this book their fullest support from the outset.

I have had help and encouragement from numerous people, although I should stress that any errors that remain in the book are entirely mine. I would like to mention the following (in alphabetical order):

Major Grant Baker, formerly Grenadier Guards; Ross Beckett; Colonel Tom Bonas, formerly Welsh Guards; Professor Brian Bond, formerly King's College London; Colonel Hugh Boscawen, formerly Coldstream Guards; Colonel Michael Craster, formerly Grenadier Guards; Mr Colin Dean, formerly Band Secretary, The Band of the Irish Guards; Gary Gibbs, The Guards Museum; Major James Greenfield, formerly Scots Guards; Professor Brian Holden-Reid, King's College London; Captain Christopher Joll, formerly The Life Guards; Major James Kelly, formerly Scots Guards; Major James Kerr, formerly Coldstream Guards; Ted Land, formerly The Life Guards, Household Cavalry Museum; Major General Anthony Leask, CB, CBE, formerly Scots Guards; Major Rupert Lendrum, formerly The Blues and Royals; John Lloyd, formerly The Life Guards, Household Cavalry Museum; Colonel Sir William Mahon, Bt, LVO, formerly Irish Guards; Peter Martin; Major Sir Fergus Matheson, Bt, formerly Coldstream Guards; Major Randall Nicol, formerly Scots Guards; Captain Alan Ogden, formerly Grenadier Guards; Captain Edward Pereira, formerly Coldstream Guards; Major Tim Pritchard-Barrett, formerly Welsh Guards; Colonel Tim Purdon, OBE, formerly Irish Guards; Guy Rasch; Major Brian Rogers, The Life Guards; Trevor Royle; Captain Roddy Sale, formerly Irish Guards; Lieutenant Colonel Harry Scott, formerly The Life Guards; Gerard Sprenger; Lieutenant Colonel Giles Stibbe, OBE, formerly The Life Guards; Major William Style, formerly Coldstream Guards; Colonel Simon Vandeleur, formerly Coldstream Guards; Captain Rhydian Vaughan, formerly Welsh Guards; Andrew Wallis, Curator, The Guards Museum; Major Ray Watson, formerly Coldstream Guards; Martin Westwood, Director, Household Cavalry Museum; Major General Peter Williams, CMG, OBE, formerly Coldstream Guards; Major Philip Wright, OBE, formerly Grenadier Guards; and Samantha Wyndham.

At Third Millennium Publishing, I would like to thank: Julian Platt, Founder; Dr Neil Titman, formerly Publishing Director; Matthew Wilson, Art Director; and Sarah McDonald, Sales and Marketing Manager.

And finally, to the team who steered the book to publication during the last few weeks of typesetting and editing, an experience that I enjoyed more than I could have expected: Neil Burkey, Publishing Director; Hannah Bowen, Editorial Project Manager; Susan Pugsley, Designer; and Patrick Taylor, Project Editor.

1914

There were two editions of the *Household Brigade Magazine* in early 1914, and neither of them mentioned any forebodings of war. As the Guards looked forward to another busy summer season of state occasions and ceremonial duties, the magazine reflected an ordered and predictable round of events. The February 1914 edition recorded the seasonal festivities two months earlier, including attempts by soldiers of 2nd Life Guards at Hyde Park Barracks 'to conceal the architectural shortcomings of their respective rooms' with Christmas decorations, the Sergeants' Smoking Concerts in the three Grenadier battalions, and the 3rd Battalion Coldstream Guards annual families' 'Christmas Tree and Entertainment' at Chelsea Barracks. On New Year's Eve, the Sergeants of 2nd Battalion Scots Guard held a Hogmanay party at the Tower of London, a 'merry' evening although many of those present 'could not boast of hailing from the land o' the heather and haggis'.

The May 1914 edition of the magazine was to be the last for five years, and there was nothing there to give any clue of what was to come a few months later. The 'regimental intelligence' section of the magazine reported mostly on competitive achievements: 'Sword versus Sword' and 'Charging Practice' for the Household Cavalry; 'Bayonet Fighting' for the Foot Guards; and for everyone plenty of running, boxing, rugby and football. Among the feature articles in the magazine was one about the fighting at Hougoumont Farm 99 years earlier on the field of Waterloo and also a short piece entitled 'The Cuirass in Modern Warfare'. It was another world, and for the Guards during that early summer, it was business as usual. On Monday 22 June, King George V was at Horse Guards for the Trooping the Colour, on the first occasion that the Sovereign led his Guards down The Mall to the Victoria Memorial rather than dismissing

1st Battalion Grenadier Guards rugby football team, 1913–14.

Above: *Men of the 1st (Royal) Dragoons at Ludgershall Camp, after returning from overseas in 1914. They were to serve alongside the Household Cavalry in the 7th Cavalry Division.*

Below: *4th Battalion Grenadier Guards, England, August 1915. Harold Macmillan is third from right, standing; on his right, Osbert Sitwell.*

them on the parade ground. *The Times* described the occasion as 'A thoughtful and popular addition' to the parade, since 'a large number of the King's subjects, for whom there was no room on Horse Guards, had a close view of their Sovereign'.

On 28 June 1914 Archduke Franz Ferdinand, heir to the throne of the Austro-Hungarian Empire, was assassinated in Sarajevo. For the British, this

Right: *Osbert Sitwell in 1911, aged 18, the year he was commissioned into the Sherwood Rangers. Soon he transferred to the Grenadier Guards, enjoying a period of ceremonial duty, along with parties, the theatre, art galleries, and being part of London's literary and cultural scene. On mobilisation, he soon found himself in the trenches close to Ypres.*

was no more than a tragic event in a troubled part of Europe where several crises had come and gone in recent years. Osbert Sitwell, a young Grenadier Guards officer serving on public duties in London, later recalled in the third volume of his autobiography, *Great Morning*, that 'Few people, especially among my brother-officers, knew anything, either of him [the Archduke] or of his place of assassination'. There were some who 'seemed oddly perturbed at the murder. It was difficult to understand why. The place, wherever it was, remained a long way off; and throughout the lives of my generation foreign royalties and heads of state had been murdered with regularity.'

In those first few days and weeks, the crisis deepened, complacency was replaced by rumours of war, mobilisation plans were dusted off, and the British Army readied itself for service overseas. Within just over a month, Europe was at war and the British Expeditionary Force (BEF) en route to France. As reality dawned, Osbert Sitwell observed a 'sudden, almost unbearable restlessness' among his fellow officers, 'young men, nearly all of whom had, a week or two before, been content with their lot, but were now experiencing an anguished desire for change'. Their plans 'were not destined to be realised. By the late autumn, they were all dead.'

A small incident on 22 July 1914 involving the Irish Guards was soon to be forgotten. Following an unsuccessful meeting at Buckingham Palace to discuss outstanding issues in the Irish Home Rule Bill, two Irish leaders, both Members of Parliament, walked past

Wellington Barracks, accompanied by a cheering group of civilians, soon joined by a small number of off-duty Irish Guardsmen. The noise attracted the attention of more soldiers leaning from their barrack windows, cheering these national heroes. The following morning, the Commanding Officer, Lieutenant Colonel the Honourable George Morris, spoke to his soldiers about the incident: 'You are all, or nearly all, racing men and like a good bet from time to time. Back what horse you like – but keep your tips to yourself.' Although it seems a minor event in comparison to the maelstrom that was to follow, at the time this small incident raised a question in the House of Commons, and a response from the Prime Minister, Herbert Asquith.

Edwardian Days

The first decade of the 20th century brought for the Guards a period of peacetime soldiering and ceremonial on a scale that had not been seen for years. The wars of the 19th century were over, and King Edward VII was on the throne, now taking on a much more active and flamboyant role as the monarch. He opened Parliament, rode on the King's Birthday Parade, hosted state visits, receptions and balls. In all of these, the Guards played an important role. The officers, as members of the Court, attended social events while they and their regiments conducted ceremonial duties in London and Windsor.

The aftermath of the South African War saw considerable changes, and when Lord Haldane became Secretary of State for War in December 1905 he began a far-reaching series of reforms that were to have an impact on training and doctrine, selection and promotion, living conditions, and the whole structure of the British Army. The year 1906 saw the concept of an expeditionary force beginning to emerge, in response to concerns about Britain's ability to contend with a future European war. In 1907 a Special Reserve designed to reinforce the Regulars in time of war, and a Territorial Force for home defence, were both formed.

Army reorganisation led to savings in equipment that would reduce the capabilities of any future expeditionary force, for example, in the supply of heavy artillery, machine guns, and infantry weapons. Manpower also suffered, and several regiments were disbanded; 3rd Battalion Scots Guards was lost and 3rd Battalion Coldstream Guards was only saved by a five-year posting to Egypt.

Taken altogether, these changes had a positive effect on the British Army, helping to develop a robust and deployable fighting force in which *esprit de corps* and regimental spirit played an important part.

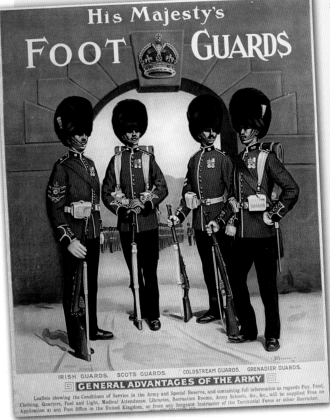

His Majesty's FOOT GUARDS

IRISH GUARDS.   SCOTS GUARDS.   COLDSTREAM GUARDS.   GRENADIER GUARDS.

GENERAL ADVANTAGES OF THE ARMY

Leaflets showing the Conditions of Service in the Army and Special Reserve, and containing full information as regards Pay, Food, Clothing, Quarters, Fuel and Light, Medical Attendance, Libraries, Recreation Rooms, Army Schools, &c., &c., will be supplied Free on Application at any Post Office in the United Kingdom, or from any Sergeant Instructor of the Territorial Force or other Recruiter.

MOBILISATION AND THE OUTBREAK OF WAR

On Tuesday 4 August 1914, during a three-day bank holiday in England, the mobilisation order went out to the regiments and units of the BEF. In HQ London District, staff officers began to contact Guards regiments serving in the London area. Just after 5pm, the Acting Regimental Adjutant of the Grenadier Guards, Captain St Leger Glyn, received the order by telephone to 'mobilise', and within two hours, all call-up telegrams to reservists had been despatched. Britain's final ultimatum to Germany expired at 11pm, and the country was now at war. The following day, a stream of former soldiers, many of whom had been on active service during the South African War, reported to mobilisation centres, some not even waiting for their telegrams to arrive.

It was an exciting time, with this rush to re-join the Colours for service at 'an unknown destination'. Frenetic preparations ensued, as medical boards were conducted;

Above: *The first contingent of 1st Life Guards ready to leave Knightsbridge Barracks. Left to right: Captain J. C. Gerard Leigh, Corporal of Horse Randle, and Corporal of Horse Horseman.*

Above top: *Reservists of the Grenadier Guards re-enlisting on the outbreak of war, queuing for a medical inspection at Wellington Barracks, 5 August 1914.*

uniforms, new boots, and kit issued; and pay parades, endless inspections, and route marches took place through the streets of London. At Wellington Barracks, with its long line of open railings running down Birdcage Walk, the gates were firmly locked as passers-by and bystanders observed the activity taking place on the huge square. On 11 August, the 1st Battalion Irish Guards was on parade for the Colonel of the Regiment, Field Marshal Lord Roberts. It was the last time they were to

Above left: *1st Life Guards ready to leave Knightsbridge Barracks.*

Above right: *Lord Roberts, VC, Colonel of the Irish Guards.*

Below left: *1st Life Guards. Some 'old dug-outs' re-join their regiment.*

see him. Looking frail, and aged nearly 82, he was to die of pneumonia three months later on a visit to France.

The photographs of the day, particularly those of the redoubtable Mrs Albert Broom, capture the fervour and enthusiasm of the Guards as they formed up on parade grounds around London. The war diary of the 1st Battalion Scots Guards on 5 August records: 'Three parties of reservists arrived [today]. Magnificent, clean, steady men'. A group of 1st Life Guards, described by Mrs Broom as 'old dug-outs', grin at the camera: men who had clearly made their way in civilian life, but were now happy to be back among old comrades and friends. The transition to war had been one of the most remarkable and well-planned mobilisations that the British Army had seen. Reservists knew who they were and had already received their railway warrants and 3-shilling postal orders; all that was needed was the telegram to 'mobilise'.

Mrs Albert Broom
PHOTOGRAPHER TO THE GUARDS

Christina Broom (whose professional name was Mrs Albert Broom) was a self-taught photographer who began her association with the Household Brigade in 1904 when she photographed a sporting event held by the Scots Guards and then sent copies to the regiment. This led to her appointment as official photographer to the Household Brigade. Selling prints to soldiers at 2d. each, with an envelope for writing home, she gained an endorsement from Lord Roberts, Colonel of the Irish Guards, who saw this as useful for recruitment in the lean years following the South African War.

In August 1914, Mrs Broom visited barracks, railway stations and makeshift encampments, taking photographs of the Guards preparing for war. The record is a unique one: families saying farewell, soldiers on their final pay parade before departing, reservists queuing up for their medical inspection, soldiers at a training camp on Wimbledon Common or on the parade ground at Wellington Barracks. There were many individual portraits, to be treasured by the families of soldiers later killed on the Western Front. There was also an informal photograph of The Prince of Wales in the uniform of a second lieutenant in the Grenadier Guards; a young, earnest-looking officer.

In all these photographs, Mrs Broom captures the excitement and apprehension during a period of heightened activity. After a long period of peace and ceremonial duties the Guards were preparing to depart for an 'unknown destination'; no one knew what to expect. Later in the war, when soldiers returned on leave, Mrs Broom was again there with her large cumbersome camera, the weight of which had briefly confined her to a wheelchair in 1915. These photographs are equally poignant, tinged perhaps with a sense of reality that was not present in August 1914. Soldiers and their families now knew what to expect as they stood together for the camera before saying goodbye; would their luck hold?

Above right: *Mrs Broom displaying her camera and examples of her photographs, Knightsbridge, May 1916.*

Left: *HRH The Prince of Wales in full war kit, Wellington Barracks, 1914.*

THE BRITISH EXPEDITIONARY FORCE

After the South African War, and following the Haldane Reforms that identified the need for an expeditionary force with the capability to deploy and sustain itself across the Channel in any future European war, the BEF, as it later came to be known, was to consist of six infantry divisions and one cavalry division. It became the focus for training in the years leading to the outbreak of war in 1914 and the nucleus for further expansion of the British Army in the months and years to follow.

The BEF in 1914 was small, around 160,000 men, but grew in size as units of the Territorial Force and contingents from around the Empire began to arrive, later to be joined by Kitchener's 'New Army'. While many of the regulars who had gone to war in 1914 had either been killed or wounded by mid-1915, by the end of the war the BEF consisted of five armies with a strength of over 2 million men.

For the Guards, there was to be a prominent role in the BEF on mobilisation, with more battalions joining in the early months of the war. Traditionally, as Household Troops, the role of the Guards was to stay close to the Sovereign during times of relative peace, avoiding long periods of routine service overseas. But in times of war, the Guards were always there – Waterloo, the Crimea and, more recently, the South African War (many veterans of that conflict were still serving in 1914 or rejoined the Colours).

On the outbreak of war, the Household Cavalry formed a Composite Regiment, with a squadron from the 1st Life Guards, 2nd Life Guards and Royal Horse Guards, as part of the 4th Cavalry Brigade, leaving for France on 13 August 1914. In the meantime, the three regiments back home were augmented by soldiers and horses of the Line Cavalry, forming the 7th Cavalry Brigade and sailing to Ostend in early October 1914. Six Foot Guards battalions were also ready, once mobilised and augmented with their reservists. The 1st Coldstream and 1st Scots Guards were

A GUARDSMAN. 1914.

Left: *A Guardsman in 1914.*

in 1st Guards Brigade, alongside 1st Black Watch and 2nd Royal Munster Fusiliers, as part of the 1st Division; while the 2nd Grenadiers, 2nd and 3rd Coldstream and 1st Irish Guards formed 4th Guards Brigade. These battalions were soon on their way to France. More, of course, were to follow, as 1st Grenadiers and 2nd Scots Guards formed up as part of 7th Division, arriving in France in October 1914.

The departure of the Guards from London was a bitter-sweet moment, as families gathered at barrack railings and railway stations, hoping to get a glimpse of their loved ones. For the soldiers, any fears and apprehensions took second place to a general sense of excitement. No one knew quite where they were going

Above: *2nd Battalion Grenadier Guards marching past Buckingham Palace, watched by King George V and other members of the Royal Family, among them the Prince of Wales, who joined 1st Battalion Grenadier Guards the following day.*

nor what they would do on arrival. Every detail of this meticulously planned mobilisation had been veiled in secrecy.

When the time came to depart, members of the Royal Family and senior officers were there to say farewell. Early on 12 August, the Irish Guards were addressed by Major General Sir Francis Lloyd, commanding London District and the Brigade of Guards, who told them to 'come back with basketfuls

The Household Cavalry in 1914

Left: *A dismounted trooper of the Royal Horse Guards, 1914.*

The Household Cavalry went to war in 1914 with the same horses that had stood on guard at Horse Guards and taken part in many state events in London and Windsor. The trooper's 'marching order' had not changed much since the South African War, although there had been some useful improvements, such as the Universal Pattern saddle, introduced in 1912. The new saddle distributed the rider's weight more evenly across the horse's back, finally resolving the problem of strength versus weight. The trooper's uniform consisted of a stiff-peaked khaki cap, a khaki serge jacket, breeches of khaki cord with leather strappings at the knees, puttees, black ankle boots and spurs. On the saddle was strapped a mess tin and feedbag containing seven pounds of oats; on the front arch were two leather wallets for miscellaneous kit, covered with a rolled mackintosh cape; while on the rear arch was a rolled raincoat.

The 1908 sword, a thrusting or pointing weapon rather than the more traditional cutting weapon, was narrower with a tapered blade and with a pistol-shaped grip designed to make it easier to hold. While it duly received Army Council approval, King George V described it as 'hideous'. He reluctantly agreed to its introduction, but insisted that the Household Cavalry would retain the 1892 pattern for ceremonial duties, the same sword that remains in use today. The 1908 sword, while slightly heavier than its predecessors, was better balanced and proved in 1914 to be effective against even the German lance. It was carried in a leather pouch suspended from a sword frog attached to the left of the saddle along with spare horse shoes, another feedbag and folding canvas bucket. Below the saddle were two blankets, one for the trooper and one for the horse.

Each soldier also carried the 1913 pattern 'short' Lee-Enfield .303 rifle in a leather rifle bucket on the right of the saddle, with 30 rounds of ammunition carried in a bandolier over the left shoulder along with a felt-covered water bottle. The rifle itself had a bolt action, a range of potentially a mile and a half, and its rate of fire was entirely down to the skill of the firer and the speed with which the small 10-round magazine could be changed. Over the trooper's right shoulder was slung a haversack 'which bulged with every sort of unauthorized contents' and around the horse's neck was a second leather bandolier with 60 rounds of ammunition.

In 1914 the regiments of the Household Cavalry went to war with a machine gun troop commanded by a subaltern, consisting of 26 all ranks and organised into two gun teams equipped with Maxim machine guns. Although the Maxim had a reasonable rate of fire at around 600 rounds a minute, and had proved its value in earlier colonial wars, it was a cumbersome and heavy weapon later to be replaced by the Vickers machine gun.

Above: Major Lord John Cavendish, DSO and Corporal Major Gulliver holding the final payday before departure for an 'unknown destination'. Knightsbridge Barracks, August 1914.

Right: Corporal of Horse J. Coates, 1st Life Guards, says farewell to his family at Nine Elms Station, August 1914.

of medals'. On 14 August, Queen Alexandra said goodbye to the Royal Horse Guards in Regent's Park, while Queen Mary did the same for the 1st Life Guards at Hyde Park. The Household Cavalry rode and the Foot Guards marched to their various embarkation points. One of them was Nine Elms Station, where plain-clothes policemen kept a wary eye out for saboteurs lurking among the soldiers' families. Lieutenant Colonel Cecil Pereira, commanding 2nd Battalion Coldstream Guards, expressed some of his feelings in a letter written to his wife: 'I am slowly realising that I am really leaving home and all that it holds. With all the business of mobilisation it is hard to realise and I felt stunned by it all.'

The Foot Guards in 1914

In August 1914, the Foot Guards wore the same khaki jacket with shoulder titles, trousers, puttees, peaked hat and brass cap badges, as the rest of the British infantry. Their webbing consisted of a belt and bayonet frog, braces with pouches for ammunition, and a pack carried high on the shoulders containing a mess kit, greatcoat, and spare clothes. A small haversack was attached to the belt when the pack was worn,

Right: *Irish Guards Machine Gun platoon, commanded by Lieutenant Eric Greer. None of these men survived the war.*

Below left: *A private in the Grenadier Guards, 1914.*

but could be carried on the back in place of the pack. A waterproof sheet was folded under the supporting straps of the pack, and a water bottle was attached to the belt. The soldier's weapon was his Short, Magazine, Lee-Enfield .303 rifle and bayonet.

Officers wore khaki jackets with badges of rank on the shoulder-straps rather than on the sleeve as was common in Line battalions, together with matching peaked hats. Dismounted officers wore cord 'ride and walk' breeches, puttees and brown ankle boots. Mounted officers wore brown leggings and ankle boots or brown field boots. All officers wore a Sam Browne belt, haversack, water bottle, field glasses, a sword and revolver. This remained the basic officer's equipment until after the First Battle of Ypres when officers replaced their swords with walking sticks.

In December 1914, goatskin jerkin coats were issued to all ranks, to be worn over the uniform but under the webbing. Although these were warm in the winter, they

made movement extremely difficult and even more so when weighed down by the mud that often hung to the goatskin hair.

Steel helmets were not worn until first introduced as an experiment during the Battle of Loos in September 1915. Helmets were issued to all troops during the following winter.

At full establishment in 1914, a Guards battalion consisted of 1,007 men, including 30 officers. It comprised a battalion headquarters and four companies, numbered 1 to 4, with the Scots Guards numbering their companies alphabetically with the right and left companies being called 'Right Flank' and 'Left Flank' respectively. The battalion was commanded by a lieutenant colonel, supported by his second-in-command, adjutant, regimental sergeant major, and quartermaster, along with a medical officer, padre, clerks, pioneers, signallers, and stretcher-bearers. Each company consisted of 227 men at full strength,

commanded by a major or captain, with a second-in-command, company sergeant major (an appointment introduced in 1914), company quartermaster sergeant, and four platoons, each commanded by a lieutenant or second lieutenant, with a platoon sergeant, and four sections, each of 12 men commanded by a corporal. After the early battles, the level of casualties dictated the size and shape of battalions and their sub-units; rarely were they at full strength for long.

Until late 1915 and the formation of the Machine Gun Companies, each battalion had a machine gun section consisting of a lieutenant, sergeant, corporal, and 14 men, equipped with two Vickers heavy machine guns manned by six-man gun teams. Transport in the battalion consisted of horses ('chargers') for the field officers, together with draught and pack horses for drawing ammunition carts, water carts, general service wagons, the medical officer's Maltese cart, and bicycles for the signallers.

The Kaiser and the Guards

Prince Wilhelm of Germany, the Crown Prince's eldest son, visited England on several occasions. He went to the theatre, watched the Eton vs Harrow cricket match and the Oxford and Cambridge Boat Race, but most of his experiences in England were of a military or naval character. He saw the Scots Guards at Windsor, later commenting in his memoirs on the 'exemplary tidiness and scrupulous cleanliness' of the barrack rooms. He was particularly taken by the uniforms: 'I am of the opinion that the pre-war British Army in its handsome peace-time uniforms was the best dressed in the world'. He also visited the 1st Life Guards, where he watched mounted training, with the finale being a musical ride, 'flawlessness executed without a word of command'.

In 1894, Queen Victoria appointed her grandson Wilhelm, now the Kaiser, as Colonel-in-Chief of the Royals. He was delighted, writing to the Queen to express 'how deeply and sincerely do I thank you for the great honour which you have conferred upon me by naming me hon. Colonel of The Royals. I am moved, deeply moved, at the idea that I can now too wear beside the naval uniform the traditional British Redcoat. How many brave and brilliant soldiers have worn it, and above all my beloved Grandpapa!'

The Kaiser invited Royals' officers to Berlin and every year presented the regiment with a wreath to commemorate Waterloo. In November 1902, he inspected the regiment at Shorncliffe on its return from the South African War, presenting German awards and making a generous donation to the families' fund. When the Royal Dragoons were posted to India

FRANCE

The Guards sailed to France in merchant marine and passenger ships. The Irish Guards, 'Thirty-two officers and close on eleven hundred rank and file, of which ninety-eight percent were Irish', departed on SS *Novara* for an uncomfortable crossing in crowded, hot and airless conditions. It was much the same for 2nd Grenadiers aboard SS *Cawdor Castle*. As

Above: *The Kaiser inspects the 1st (Royal) Dragoons at Shorncliffe on 8 November 1902.*

Left: *The Kaiser, Colonel of the 1st (Royal) Dragoons (who amalgamated with the Royal Horse Guards in 1969), wearing the uniform of his regiment.*

in 1904, the Kaiser protested to his cousin Edward VII at 'his' regiment being sent to such an uncivilised part of the world, but it went anyway.

On the outbreak of war in 1914, the Kaiser's appointment as Colonel-in-Chief came abruptly to an end, although it is said that during the war the Kaiser continued to send letters of condolence to the families to those Royals' soldiers killed. Many years later in the 1930s, the eccentric Alfred Wintle irritated his fellow Royals' officers by sending Christmas cards to the ex-Kaiser, now in exile in Holland, and displaying those that the former Colonel-in-Chief sent in return.

Above: *A horse being unloaded, Le Havre, August 1914.*

Major 'Ma' Jeffreys, Grenadier Guards, records in his diary, no one knew where they were bound, not even the ship's captain, until actually under way. When they finally set sail at 8pm, 'it was a lovely night, with not a ripple on the water, which was just as well, as it would have been remarkably unpleasant with so many men on board had it been rough'. For the Household Cavalry, in SS *Thespis*, the additional challenge of embarking with many horses made for a difficult passage.

On arrival in France, the Guards were greeted with great excitement by the French civilians. As they marched through the narrow and steep streets that led from the docks at Le Havre, they began to feel some of the weariness of the last few weeks. 'I shall never forget that march to my dying day,' recorded 'Ma' Jeffreys; 'it was the hottest march I have ever done and hope ever shall'. It was a good preparation for the challenges that were to come.

In the meantime, the Germans were advancing rapidly through Belgium, although for most of the soldiers of the BEF there was little awareness of this, or of the dangers ahead. By 16 August, the German siege of Liège had ended with the capture of the last great forts surrounding the city. The Germans were now on the move, and the gallant Belgians fighting along the Belgian–German border had almost certainly given the BEF more time to shake out and deploy into the 70-mile gap between Le Cateau and the Channel, on the left flank of the French Fifth Army. This stretch of the front was mostly undefended, with just a few isolated French territorial troops and the occasional cavalry patrol in the area.

By 20 August, the leading BEF battalions and units were in their concentration areas, poised to begin the march towards Mons, although, as 'Ma' Jeffreys noted in his diary that day, 'No one knows anything about the general situation'. The following morning the Guards were on the move, by foot, and it was a hard and gruelling march in hot weather. By 22 August, the Grenadiers had reached La Longueville and, as 'Ma' Jeffreys observed, while 'The Battalion had marched well . . . some of the reservists are not

really fit and find their heavy packs very trying in the heat. Also their new boots are not properly broken in [and there] are some sore feet [from marching on the pavé roads]'. At dawn on the same day, the BEF made its first contact with the enemy in the village of Casteau when a patrol of the 4th Royal Irish Dragoon Guards encountered a section of German Uhlans. It was here that the first British shot was fired in earnest and the first German was killed by a British soldier, by a thrust of a cavalry sword. Elsewhere, there was a sense of unreality, as Cecil Pereira observed in a letter to his wife: 'This country is typically English and it is hard to realise that we are not on manoeuvres; no doubt shortly we shall find it easy enough to realise. We have heard the sound of guns like we used to in Sussex, a long way off.'

THE RETREAT FROM MONS

The Battle of Mons, on 23 August, was the first major battle in which the BEF was engaged. It was a heroic and fierce engagement during which the much larger German First Army was briefly stopped in its advance by British units holding a line of shallow and hastily constructed trenches along the Mons–Condé Canal. 4th Guards Brigade played only a supporting role that day, with the Grenadiers and Irish Guards in reserve behind the Royal Irish Rifles. But the day was not entirely uneventful. As the Irish Guards lay in their shallow trenches, they heard the battle raging to their front. 'It was as though a scythe of rifle fire and machine-gun bullets was passing directly over their heads. It came in gusts, whistling, snarling, sighing. "This is Hell Fire" said one [guardsman]; a good few were praying or crossing themselves'.

The Battle of Mons was short and sharp but could never have been a British victory. Retreat was inevitable, given the size and ferocity of the German attack and the weakness of the BEF's flanks. But neither was it a defeat. This 'contemptible little army', as described by the Kaiser on 19 August 1914, had stood steady that day, with its riflemen firing so rapidly and accurately that some Germans believed they were facing sustained machine-gun fire. The BEF was now forced to retreat, pursued by a strong German army. For everyone, including the Guards, it was to be a l ong and hard march.

For the Household Cavalry the retreat was a 'fortnight of almost total confusion' which began with four days of skirmishes with the advancing Germans. Then, on 27 August the Composite Regiment was ordered to lead the withdrawal, with no idea of what lay ahead. There were few opportunities to stop and rest. As one trooper described, 'the men slept in their saddles and were wakened at intervals by their neighbours; the horses slouched along mechanically on the heels of those in front'.

Left: *The Household Cavalry Composite Regiment on the Retreat from Mons, August 1914.*

Major Lord Bernard Gordon-Lennox
COMMANDING NO. 2 COMPANY, 2ND BATTALION GRENADIER GUARDS

DIARY EXTRACT

24th August 1914. 'Off again at daybreak and saw the Germans simply pounding the ridge we had evacuated. As the infantry would probably shortly be up there, and find out we had left, and send word, and as we were in full view of the bridge, we lost no time in getting out of our unenviable position. This began our long and tiring retirement, beginning at Mons and

finishing up near Paris, and I don't think any of us wish to go through such a trying time again. Also the British Army is not accustomed to retiring. To revert. We retired about 2 miles to Quévy-le-Grand where we reached about 6 a.m. and received orders to dig ourselves in, and fight a rear-guard action. We had hardly arrived there, when the German shells began dropping on the last place we had evacuated. We afterwards heard they turned 15 batteries on it and pounded it up to mincemeat for 3 hours, so it was lucky we left. We could see the shells bursting just ahead of us. Gunning was going on or around, and it looked as if our flanks were being turned. Owing to the absolute secrecy which pervaded everything, no one knew what was going on anywhere: this has been maintained up to date and is most disheartening. No one knows what one is driving at, where anyone is, what we have got against us, or anything at all, and what is told us generally turns out to be entirely wrong'.

Bernard Gordon-Lennox was killed on 10 November 1914. As recorded in the Regimental Diary:

A heavy loss this day was the death of Major Lord Bernard Gordon-Lennox, who was killed by a high explosive shell. For three months he had been in the thick of every engagement, always cheerful, and always making the best of every hardship. He was one of the most popular officers in the Brigade of Guards and his death was very keenly felt by everyone.

LANDRECIES

By the late afternoon of 25 August, 4th Guards Brigade had reached the small town of Landrecies on the River Sambre, following a fitful few hours of sleep the previous night and a long march that had begun around 3am. But any hope of a peaceful night's rest was in vain, since the Germans were on their heels, the outskirts of the town needed to be picqueted, and the roads fortified with makeshift barricades. The brigade quickly took up positions, with 3rd Coldstream at the northern end of the town, 2nd Grenadiers on the western side, 2nd Coldstream on the eastern and southern outskirts of the town, and 1st Irish Guards in the centre.

Charles 'Budget' Loyd, Coldstream Guards, recalled,

> Late in the afternoon of 25 August we enter Landrecies, hot and exhausted . . . I get my men into quite a good place, arrange for their food and go off to find that I have been allotted a nice room with a good bed at the top of a women's clothes shop. It is full of girls who are clearly frightened and apprehensive. I manage to persuade one to produce a hip-bath with some hot water, into which I get with relief but with smarting blisters and I start to wash myself properly. Suddenly shots ring down the street and I hear the whizz of bullets outside. The girls rush into my room in a panic and the sight of me in my bath does nothing to calm them. I leap out, dress more quickly than I have ever dressed before and, expecting orders, re-join my platoon, but it is a false alarm.

The Germans were definitely on their way, and at around 7pm, as dusk was falling, they arrived in strength, launching the first of several attacks against the Coldstreamers. Sometime in the early hours the area was illuminated by a burning haystack that made the Coldstream position vulnerable to a German field gun firing at short range up the road. Private George Wyatt crossed the open ground to extinguish the flames while under fire from the enemy. Following another act of bravery a week later at Villers-Cotterêts, he was awarded the Victoria Cross (VC) for both actions.

The Germans now managed to outflank 3rd Coldstream's position as far as the railway station where they were repelled by 2nd Grenadiers. The German field gun was destroyed by a howitzer from the supporting battery and, meanwhile, 1st Irish Guards launched a counter-attack in the east of the town at around 3am. Losing momentum, the German attacks ceased before dawn, 3rd Coldstream were relieved by 1st Irish Guards and, in the dull light of the early morning, 4th Guards Brigade marched safely out of Landrecies heading south. But the

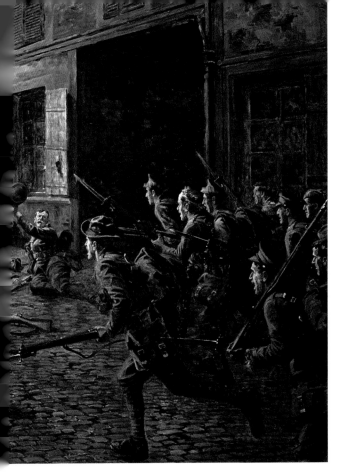

Germans were not far behind, and occupied the town as the brigade's field ambulance was collecting the British wounded.

The Coldstream Guards had taken the brunt of the attacks on the town, and it had been a bloody affair, fought not from trenches but in the streets and around the corners of the houses. Field Marshal Sir John French, Commander-in-Chief BEF, in his first dispatch of the war to be published in the *London Gazette*, described the action:

> Well and truly did the Coldstreamers play their allotted part through that terrible night. Some lay across the streets, others worked machine-guns in sheltered positions, while others rushed forward and drove their bayonets into the enemy, all being under a steady fire from the guns brought up by the Germans in the dark.

This had all taken place at close quarters, much of it hand to hand and with bayonets. During the fighting, 3rd Coldstream had lost 2 officers and 12 soldiers killed, with a further 108 wounded and 11 missing. 2nd Grenadier Guards lost 1 officer killed and 6 soldiers wounded.

On the scale of what was to come in the next few months, Landrecies was no more than a skirmish. But it was the first major engagement for the Guards in the war and, more importantly, the action possibly saved much of the Headquarters of Lieutenant General Sir Douglas Haig's I Corps, which had been billeted in the town.

4th Guards Brigade continued on the march to the south and on 30 August passed another brigade resting by the roadside. Without any order being given, the Guardsmen braced themselves, unslung their rifles, sloped arms, and began marching to the steady beat of their regimental marches played on mouth organs. They marched 'as if they were on Guard Mounting', and it was 'an intensely moving and uplifting experience for those who witnessed it'.

The routine of marching continued for the next few days, to the extent that it had become 'curiously normal'. Every hour, there was a 10-minute halt for rest, with every man not on guard duty immediately lapsing into sleep. When they began marching again, the files were changed so that those that had been on the verge were now on the camber of the pavé. Each had its own discomforts: the unevenness of the cobble or the dust of the gutter. The men were very tired and while most kept going, one or two dropped out along the way.

Second Lieutenant Robert Vereker
THE FIRST GRENADIER OFFICER TO DIE IN THE WAR

2nd Grenadiers saw serious action for the first time at Landrecies on the night of 25 August 1914. During the fighting, the German troops had managed to get near the railway station and fire on No. 2 Company commanded by Major Lord Bernard Gordon-Lennox, who later recalled that 'Bullets began to whisk past us and it was just about at this time that poor young Vereker was shot dead through the head'.

Robert Vereker joined the regiment in 1913, aged 20, and was to be the first of 203 Grenadier officers to be killed in the war. His parents were informed of his death in two telegrams from the War Office preprinted with the words 'Deeply regret to inform you'. The padre, the Reverend B. G. O'Rorke, wrote to Mr Vereker on 30 August: 'Your brave son met his death on 25th August, while trying to draw Corporal Bacchus of his regiment, who was wounded, out of range of the German line. The Corporal is now convalescent. Your son was buried in the next grave to some officers and eight men of the Coldstream Guards. We erected a rough cross giving their names. The following day the wife of the Garde Cimetière brought me a cross of a more substantial kind, and I left instructions for their names to be painted on it. It was her own thought and her own tribute'. The Committee of Adjustment convened on 17 December found that Robert Vereker had no liabilities, his only assets being the contents of his field kit, purchased by him from the Wilkinson Sword Company for £5 15 shillings, and consisting of a compactum bed, hair pillow, bath/wash bucket, chair, groundsheet and kitbag. His father, as executor, requested reimbursement for the field kit from the War Office and this was paid in April 1915.

In memory of their son, the Verekers lent their house near Salcombe for use as a Red Cross convalescent home. The inscription on Robert Vereker's grave in the Communal Cemetery at Landrecies, chosen by his father, reads 'I shall be with you when the light shines and in the darkness I shall not forget'.

VILLERS-COTTERÊTS

On the evening of 31 August 1914, 4th Guards Brigade halted close to Villers-Cotterêts, just north of the Forêt de Retz. They had now been marching in hot weather for over a week with little sleep and having fought a battle at Landrecies. With an expected German attack from the north, the brigade was now ordered to form a rearguard to cover the withdrawal of the 2nd Division. 2nd Grenadiers and 3rd Coldstream dug hasty defensive positions about 1 mile to the north of the forest, a company was detached to protect the left flank, and 1st Irish Guards and 2nd Coldstream were placed in support on the northern edge of the trees.

During the early hours of 1 September, 2nd Division marched through the Guards' positions, towards Villers-Cotterêts. The following morning, the two forward Guards battalions withdrew about 1 mile into the forest to Le Rond de la Reine, where the road sweeps in a semi-circular direction and meets one of the rides through the forest. Here 2nd Grenadiers and 3rd Coldstream took up positions, very close to where a Guards memorial now stands. At about 10am, an advance guard of German cavalry, infantry and artillery arrived on the edge of the forest, attacking 1st Irish Guards and 2nd Coldstream. Returning fire, and with the support of British field guns, the Guards brought the advance temporarily to a halt. The time had now come to withdraw, and with the Coldstream already beginning their move, Lieutenant Colonel the Honorable George Morris of the Irish Guards was ordered to hold his position while 2nd Division just to the south rested for a few hours. But very soon the enemy were upon the Guards, with infantry of the German 5th and 6th Divisions attacking their hasty positions, making swift advances along the rides that criss-cross the forest.

Above: *Lieutenant Colonel the Honourable George Morris.*

This was not a good place for a battle, for either side. It was unfamiliar, the wood was dense and fields of fire were limited as rifle rounds ricocheted around the forest. Soon it was impossible to know friend from foe, as the fighting amongst the trees became chaotic. The Brigade Commander, Brigadier General Scott-Kerr, attempted to extend his line to the west to block the Germans, but it was too late. The Irish Guards fell back to the main position around Le Rond de la Reine. Unit cohesion among the Guards battalions had now been virtually lost, with officers and non-commissioned officers taking command of anyone they could see. A German machine gun firing down one of the long diagonal rides caused many casualties and, to make matters worse, the Brigade Commander had now been

Right: *The memorial to the Grenadier, Coldstream and Irish Guardsmen killed or mortally wounded during the rearguard action at Villers-Cotterêts commissioned by Lady Edward Cecil and unveiled in 1922.*

Below: *2nd Lieutenant George Cecil, Grenadier Guards.*

badly wounded and evacuated. Lieutenant Colonel Noel Corry, commanding 2nd Grenadier Guards, took over the brigade while Major 'Ma' Jeffreys assumed command of the battalion.

By midday, two platoons of 2nd Grenadiers had been cut off and overrun, fighting to the end. The brigade had suffered heavy losses in just a few hours of bitter and confused fighting. The Grenadiers lost 4 officers and 160 men; the Coldstream, 3 officers and 37 men; the Irish Guards, 9 officers and 115 men, including their Commanding Officer, George Morris.

PASSANT

ARRETE-TOI

Following the battle, the local people from Villers-Cotterêts buried many of the soldiers in the forest, close to Le Rond de la Reine where the most intensive fighting had taken place.

Lady Edward Cecil, whose son George, a Grenadier officer, was killed at Villers-Cotterêts, visited the area just a few weeks after the fighting in a vain attempt to find her son's grave. In November 1914, Lord Killanin, the brother of Lieutenant Colonel George Morris, came for another search and found a mass grave. His party set about the unpleasant task of exhuming the bodies:

Lance Corporal George Wyatt, VC

COLDSTREAM GUARDS

The First Guards' Victoria Cross of the War

George Henry Wyatt was born in 1886 at Whistones, Worcester. He enlisted into the Coldstream Guards in November 1904, serving with 2nd and 3rd Battalions at home and in Egypt. Discharged in November 1908, he joined the Barnsley Borough Police Force, followed by the Doncaster Police Force from May 1914. As a reservist, he was called up on 5 August 1914 and posted to 3rd Battalion Coldstream Guards, leaving for France a few days later.

George Wyatt was awarded the VC for his heroism during the fighting at Landrecies and Villers-Cotterêts. His citation, published in the *London Gazette*, reads: 'on the night of 25–26 August, 1914, when a part of his Battalion was hotly engaged at the end of a street close to some farm buildings, the enemy, by means of incendiary bombs, set light to some straw stacks in the farmyard. Lance Corporal Wyatt twice dashed out of the line under very heavy fire from the enemy, who were only 25 yards distant, and extinguished the burning straw. If the fire had spread it would have been quite impossible to have held our position. Also at Villers-Cotterêts, after being wounded in the head, Lance Corporal Wyatt continued firing until he could no longer see owing to the blood which was pouring down his face. The Medical Officer bound up his wound and told him to go to the rear, but he at once returned to the firing-line and continued to fight'.

George Wyatt served on throughout the war, and was finally discharged in the rank of Lance Sergeant in early 1919. He returned to the Doncaster Police Force, and retired in 1934. He died on 22 January 1964, aged 77, and is buried at Dadeby Cemetery, Sprotbrough, Yorkshire.

in no case was it possible to identify a body by features – hair, teeth, as owing to the length of time (two and a half months) since burial and to the manner in which these dead had been treated, the faces were quite unrecognisable, often smashed, and were all thickly coated with clay and blood.

He did, however, manage to identify his brother's remains from an inscribed wristwatch, and George Cecil was identified by the initials G.E.C. embroidered on his vest. Thereafter, the cemetery was properly marked and later taken over by the Imperial War Graves Commission. A memorial, unveiled in 1922 and commissioned by Lady Edward Cecil, stands close to the cemetery and on the corner of the road at Le Rond de la Reine. It commemorates all those Guardsmen who died at Villers-Cotterêts, with special mention of George Cecil, who was aged 18 when he was killed.

THE MARNE
AND THE AISNE

By 30 August, the Household Cavalry had reached Compiègne without seeing much of the enemy except for a brief encounter with some German Uhlans the previous day. Their first real clash with the enemy came two days later near the village of Néry. On 1 September, with the ground thick with fog, breakfast was interrupted by 'bullets whizzing overhead out of the mist, and the roar of guns increased in volume every minute'. Soon 4th Cavalry Brigade was saddled up and riding towards the sound of the artillery. Somehow, although no one knew it at the time, a German cavalry advance guard, along with its guns, had managed to get through the British lines in the darkness and mist. Soon, a dismounted attack was ordered by the German Divisional Commander, supported by artillery firing from the high ground. In the fighting that followed, 'L' Battery, Royal Horse Artillery took heavy casualties and was left with just one gun firing, a brave action that was later to lead to the award of three VCs. With the British Cavalry now in place, the Germans' luck turned as they were effectively surrounded. The Household Cavalry, on the high ground, was out of the firing line, but only just, as the regimental historian recorded: 'The Blues stood in a rich clover field and watched three German machine guns mow a path across their front, the closer falling as though cut by a giant scythe.' Then Lieutenant 'Volley' Heath was sent forward with his troop 'on to some ground partly hidden by a haystack, where he espied a considerable party of the enemy and, without more ado, charged them'. The enemy counter-attacked and, in the

act of pulling back with his men and horses, Heath was hit several times and then in the head. He later died in hospital, the first Household Cavalry fatality of the war.

Then, on 5 September, the retreat was halted, and the BEF was ordered to march northwards. As 'Budget' Loyd described it,

> we are told we are to march back the way we have come. It is literally a case of 'About turn, Quick march'. Knowing nothing of the general situation, we are completely mystified as to what is happening. Later we learn that the great retreat is over, and that we are now pushing the enemy back.

Right: *Captain H. C. 'Budget' Loyd in 1915, wearing his three wound stripes on his lower sleeve. He joined the Coldstream in 1910 at the time of the passing of Lloyd George's 'People's Budget', hence his nickname.*

The Germans had been on the advance for a month, had now overextended themselves, and the chance for the Allies to strike back had arrived. What followed was the Battle of the Marne, during which the French Army, supported by the BEF, stopped the Germans along the line of the River Marne and began to push them back towards the River Aisne, a distance of 60 miles.

The advance began south of the Marne, as the Allies closed up on the Germans. On the way north, on 8 September, 4th Guards Brigade, joined now by 1st Guards Brigade, took part in an action to force a river crossing at the Petit Morin, a tributary of the main river. German snipers hid in the trees, picking off officers, identifying them by the gold braid on their peaked hats. During the action, 2nd Coldstream captured 3 officers, some 90 soldiers and 6 machine guns. The Irish Guards,

now in reserve, took over the prisoners, and invited German officers to dinner, with the 'niceties of war . . . still being observed'.

The Marne was crossed on 9 September and over the next three days the BEF advanced a further 30 miles. Five days later they were on the banks of the Aisne. It was here that 1st Guards Brigade was involved in its first major action of the war when it attacked up the steep wooded northern bank of the river, across the plateau to the Chemin des Dames, a road running along a prominent ridge, so named because it followed a route taken by two of Louis XV's daughters in the 18th century. It was a formidable obstacle: Napoleon had defeated Blücher here a

Private Frederick Dobson, VC

COLDSTREAM GUARDS

Frederick William (Billy) Dobson was born in 1886, and joined the Coldstream Guards in 1906. He was discharged exactly three years later, and then mobilised on 6 August 1914, joining the 2nd Battalion. Then, on 28 September, at Chavonne, north of the River Aisne, he exposed himself to heavy fire on two occasions to rescue wounded men. His Commanding Officer, Lieutenant Colonel Cecil Pereira, in a letter to his wife, wrote 'I have today recommended one of our private soldiers for the Victoria Cross. I hope for his sake and of the Regiment they will award it . . . . A most gallant action'. Sir Douglas Haig did not agree, expressing in a note dated 30 September the view that he was 'not in favour of this coveted award being created for bringing in wounded officers or men in European warfare'. Instead, he recommended the DCM; however, the King overruled him. Dobson's award was gazetted on 9 December, and he received his medal from the King at Buckingham Palace on 3 February 1915. His citation, published in the *London Gazette*, reads:

> For conspicuous gallantry at Chavonne (Aisne) on the 28 September, in bringing into cover on two occasions, under heavy fire, wounded men who were lying exposed in the open.

Lance Corporal Dobson was discharged from the Army in July 1917 as 'no longer physically fit for war service'. He suffered from constant pain from shrapnel wounds which continued for the remainder of his life. A combination of his wounds and the burden of his VC gave him no favours as he attempted to seek work in the mines. He said that 'the miners made it tough for me', claiming that he received special treatment from the management. He then found work as a cinema commissionaire, living in Leeds, later moving into rooms in Newcastle. The pain from his war wounds persisted, and he spent many months in and out of hospital, and it was here, in Newcastle, that he died on 13 November 1935, aged 49. He was buried at Ryton Cemetery, Gateshead, Tyne and Wear.

Three of his five medals, including the VC, were found in a Newcastle pawnbrokers shop in 1936. In accordance with the Dobson family wishes, the medals were returned to the regiment. In 1988 the wife of Frederick Dobson's eldest son, who had died three months earlier, wrote to Regimental Headquarters to say that she had the two other medals, the British War Medal and the Victory Medal. These had belonged to her husband who had always intended that they be given to the regiment.

Frederick Dobson's story is a sad one: he was a man of great courage who had been awarded the highest honour for saving the lives of others, and yet his VC brought him little, if any, happiness.

Right: *Private William Hards, 1st Battalion, Scots Guards. Fought and was wounded on the Aisne. Died of his wounds in 1915.*

century earlier, and now the Guards were fighting an engagement described by the Brigade Commander, Brigadier General Ivor Maxse, as 'a ding-dong battle under heavy German artillery fire to which our gunners could not then reply. The result was that we lost about one third of my brigade in killed, wounded and missing in about a couple of hours or so.' But the brigade held its ground, gaining 'an indispensable bridgehead over the river'. Just before midday, 1st Coldstream managed to cross the Chemin des Dames, but were later surrounded and forced to withdraw under cover of darkness. The battalion sustained losses of 388 on that day alone.

At the same time, 4th Guards Brigade was engaged further west, to capture the well-defended La Cour de Soupir Farm, just north of the village of Soupir, in a prominent position on the plateau above the Aisne. It was to be bitter fighting, during which 2nd Coldstream sustained 66 men killed and wounded. It was here, on 28 September, that Private Frederick Dobson volunteered to cross exposed ground under heavy fire and in daylight to rescue two wounded comrades. Having covered a considerable distance, he found one soldier dead and the other lying injured. Dressing the wounds, he made his way back, returning with a stretcher and another soldier, Corporal Brown. Together, they managed to get the wounded man back to safety. Dobson was awarded the VC, and Brown received the Distinguished Conduct Medal (DCM).

The brief advance following the Battle of the Marne was now drawing to a close, the Germans having recovered themselves sufficiently to establish strong defensive positions, mostly on ground that gave them all the advantages of a defender. It was to be a significant turning point: both sides were constructing some of the first trenches of the war, and a new phase was about to begin. Over the next few weeks the Guards remained above the Aisne, establishing a kind of routine that was to be all too familiar in the months and years to come. Companies took it in turns to occupy the front line of trenches, alternating with a supporting role. Frequent artillery shelling and machine-gun fire along the front made movement beyond the trenches impossible during daytime.

The Aisne, September 1914

By early September 1914, 2nd Grenadiers had taken part in the retreat to the Marne followed by the cautious pursuit of the German Army to the Aisne, where the enemy was now digging-in above the steep and wooded slopes of the river valley. Gradually, under intensive shelling, the trenches were improved and made deeper, and rabbit netting found nearby became wire entanglements. Raids were conducted to stalk the enemy's snipers hidden in trees, haystacks and wood stacks which had been hollowed out, the Germans often mistaking the rapid fire of the .303 rifle for machine guns. In one patrol, Lance Corporal P. H. McDonnell with two men reconnoitred a small wood a few hundred yards in front of the front line. They discovered a party of about 30 Germans in an advanced trench at the forward edge who thought they had captured the patrol but then took heavy casualties when McDonnell ordered his two soldiers to open fire. The three Grenadiers escaped, and McDonnell was awarded the DCM. He later transferred to the Welsh Guards and was promoted to sergeant.

Another three-man patrol, led by Lance Corporal W. Thomas, tasked to go through a wood to burn a wood stack from which sniping had been taking place, met a group of 15 Germans who they managed to drive off before lighting the wood stack. Thomas, badly hit in the action, was awarded the DCM and later promoted to sergeant. Both Thomas and McDonnell were presented with their medal ribbons by the King on a visit in early December 1914. Thomas was killed in the trenches on Christmas Eve 1914; an extract from a letter sent to his sister by the men of 4 Platoon of No. 1 Company reads: 'He was killed instantly by a shot in the head on the afternoon of 24 December. It may be a relief to you to know that he died fighting to the last. The Germans were in our trenches and he barred the way shooting down every man that came his way. He saved many of us and we greatly sympathise with you in your loss'.

Right: *Bridge over the River Aisne where 4th Guards Brigade crossed, September 1914.*

THE FIRST BATTLE OF YPRES

Field Marshal Sir John French was not happy with the BEF dispositions along the Aisne. His lines of communication from England had been stretched and he was not best placed to defend Antwerp and the all-important Channel Ports. The French Commander-in-Chief, Maréchal Joseph Joffre, agreed to a BEF move to Flanders, provided that British units were available for operations on arrival. At the beginning of October, under the cover of darkness and in great secrecy, British units began the move northwards, on foot and by train. It was a complicated redeployment, as the BEF extricated itself from between the Fifth and Sixth French Armies, crossing the French lines of communication.

2nd Coldstream were finally relieved on the Aisne by a reserve battalion of the French Army on 13 October. Cecil Pereira, writing home to his wife, recorded his first impressions:

> Our French relief arrived without transport or food or extra ammunition; all rather sketchy according to our ideas. They were very much struck with our men, with their physique and bearing. Our clothing also

and the men's rations, and cookers were a source of wonder. They were most grateful for luncheon, five of them were able to come; it happened to be an extra good luncheon, among other dishes macaroni and eggs, stewed pears and rice, also Cointreau, whiskey, rum and cigars, also butter. They have the impression that we live like fighting cocks. As a matter of fact we don't do badly.

If anyone was hoping for a quieter time in Flanders, closer to home and perhaps a little safer, they were to be disappointed. On 9 October Antwerp fell to the Germans, and there was now a possibility that they would encircle the Allies. With stalemate setting in elsewhere on a front line that stretched from the North Sea to the Alps, the Germans had decided to concentrate their efforts in Flanders and particularly around Ypres.

Above top: St Jacob's Church and houses destroyed by shellfire, Ypres.

Left: On the road from Roulers (Roeselare) to Ypres. Inhabitants giving hot coffee to men of 2nd Scots Guards, 14 October 1914.

Lieutenant Colonel Cecil Pereira
COMMANDING OFFICER, 2ND BATTALION COLDSTREAM GUARDS

LETTER TO HIS WIFE

8th October 1914 – Chavonne. 'I will give you my daily routine. This morning Mass at 7.30 and some others went to the sacraments. 8.30 breakfast. After that orders and various matters to attend to, distribution of clothing, socks and gifts to the battalion. 11 am COs to see the Brigadier. After that letter writing. Geoffrey Feilding [Senior CO in the Brigade] came to lunch at 12.15 pm. After that look at papers, more letters to write thanking people for socks etc., 3.30 pm on outposts and tea at the Cave at 4 pm. A tour around the outpost line inspecting work and planning new work for the night or the morrow. Dinner 7.30 pm. Round to various parts of the line. At night there are sometimes attacks near or far far off, and sometimes it's necessary to have an extra platoon in hand to reinforce any part of my line that might be attacked. 4:30 am stand to arms and so on. Some days like today, there is a holy calm. It depends very largely on aeroplane reconnaissance on both sides. The aeroplanes discover the positions of batteries, troops constructing works or on the move and then the game begins. The other side gets annoyed and tries to keep down the fire of the opposite artillery and enter heart and soul into the game. It spoils one's afternoon slumbers and injures the roofs of the village and makes circumlocution insecure. As a finale, on both sides, the artillery imagine they have utterly destroyed each other, but as the game goes on for weeks there is some mistake in their calculations.'

1st and 4th Guards Brigades were now moving north to Flanders, together with the Household Cavalry Composite Regiment which had also taken part in the long retreat from Mons, mounted throughout. In the meantime, more Guards battalions had been mobilised, were beginning to arrive in Flanders, and were digging trenches.

The three regiments of the Household Cavalry, depleted by the formation of the Composite Regiment in August, had now been reinforced by Line Cavalry Regiments (Dragoons to the 1st Life Guards, Lancers to the 2nd Life Guards, and Hussars to the Royal Horse Guards – the Blues). Forming the 7th (Household Cavalry) Brigade, they arrived at Zeebrugge on 8 October and two weeks later found themselves in trenches to the south-east of Ypres, alongside the Composite Regiment.

As part of the Cavalry Corps they were now responsible for a 35-mile frontage, with each cavalry brigade assigned to approximately 600 yards on a semicircle east of Ypres, a new scenario for cavalrymen.

The Household Cavalry still had their horses, but their role, as described by Corporal of Horse Robert Lloyd of 1st Life Guards, had become 'the rapid conveyance of rifle and bayonet soldiers to the line. The exciting scampering along country roads and through villages gave place to an existence comparable only to that of a water rat in a swamp'. With most of the soldiers in the trenches, there were only a few available behind the lines to care for the horses. Often, they remained tied up on temporary horse lines, exposed to the elements, and without proper exercise and food. Sir Morgan Crofton, an officer serving with 2nd Life

Far left: *Horse lines, 1914.*

Left: *Lieutenant Colonel Lord Tweedmouth, Royal Horse Guards.*

Guards, described the conditions in his diary:

> The horses stand about all over the place looking miserable. They have had no hay and gnaw everything they can get hold of. There is not a tree which has not yet had its bark gnawed off as high as a horse can reach, and a waggon stands just outside our door which is half eaten by them, one side entirely and half the other.

Captain Julian Grenfell, who had joined the 1st (Royal) Dragoons in 1910, was now in Flanders with his regiment, and briefly out of the line in billets and thoroughly enjoying the experience, as he described in a letter to his mother: 'It is all the most *wonderful* fun; better fun than one could ever imagine. I hope it goes on a nice long time; but pigsticking will be the only tolerable pursuit after this or one will die of sheer ennui'.

There were the occasional minor cavalry actions. Corporal of Horse Lloyd recalled a skirmish with a small detachment of Uhlans in the village of Gheluwe on 14 October that led to a 'particularly nasty' dismounted engagement' in which 'the bullets ricocheted off the cobblestones and performed ugly tricks'. Two Uhlans escaped. One made it to his horse, and galloped away,

only to be shot dead by a Royal Inniskilling Dragoon Guard attached to the squadron at a range of 1,200 yards. The other ran away on foot but was soon overtaken: 'A wild fellow, named Bellingham, of the "Skins", galloped at him and ran him through the body with his sword. He then calmly wiped his sword on the horse's mane and remarked: "That's the way to serve them bastards."'

Two weeks later, on 25 October, the Blues were ordered to make a mounted diversionary attack by riding across the front of two German cavalry regiments to help extricate 20th Infantry Brigade from Kruiseecke. One squadron dismounted on the ridge, opening fire, whilst two squadrons galloped on to outflank the German advance. The Germans then turned on the Blues, but they managed to withdraw with the loss of 8 men and 25 horses, having achieved their mission. Lord Tweedmouth recorded the events in his diary:

> Went off at the gallop, to make a demonstration, C Squadron in advance. My sword carried away just as we got to the crest between Hugh Grosvenor's trench and Gerry Ward's. We got the shrapnel pretty hot then, and my horse was shot in the leg and I had to stop and get into Hugh's trench. Got out presently and shot my horse with my revolver and saved all my kit.

GHELUVELT

1st Guards Brigade arrived in Poperinghe, 7 miles west of Ypres, on 20 October, and early the next morning took over their shallow trenches on a forward slope facing north between Bixschoote and Langemark. The Brigade was heavily shelled on 22 October, and defeated a strong infantry attack that afternoon. On 23 October, by which time the line had been mostly restored, the Germans attacked Langemark again, this time with young students advancing through the mist singing 'Deutschland über alles' and drinking songs. When the rapid 'fifteen rounds a minute' rifle fire of 1st Guards Brigade began, it was to have a devastating effect, with each rifleman firing some 500 rounds that day. German casualties were huge, the battle later becoming known as *Das Kindermord von Ypern*, the 'Massacre of the Innocents at Ypres'.

On 27 October, following a brief respite, 1st Guards Brigade redeployed to new positions east of Gheluvelt village, in the area of the Nieuwe Kruiseecke crossroads. The trenches were basic and although fields of fire were good, with up to 800 metres in clear visibility, frontages were again stretched: 1st Coldstream were covering

Above: *A German prisoner being brought in at Gheluvelt.*

Opposite top: *Major (Quartermaster) Jock Boyd, MC, after the war.*

Opposite below: *Officers of 2nd Battalion, Scots Guards preparing for a reconnaissance towards Gheluvelt, 20 October 1914.*

about 1,100 yards with a strength of only 16 officers and around 340 men.

The attack on the crossroads came at 5.30am on 29 October, in thick fog. The British artillery, short of ammunition, had been allocated only nine rounds per gun per day. By 7am, six German battalions, with a numerical superiority of around 5 to 1, were advancing through the mist towards the Coldstreamers. One company north of the crossroads was virtually destroyed, while another only succumbed once all its officers had been killed. The remaining Coldstreamers fought on with the Scots Guards, achieving some success, while the Coldstream Battalion HQ was overrun at around 8am.

By the end of that day, 1st Guards Brigade had suffered 1,100 casualties, being left with only 275

all ranks. 1st Coldstream had lost all but one of its officers, and the Quartermaster, Lieutenant Jock Boyd, could only muster around 80 men that evening. 1st Grenadiers lost 470 officers and men that day, while 2nd Scots Guards had lost 370 killed and wounded. Sir John French, in his despatch published on 30 November 1914, described the fighting at Gheluvelt as 'Perhaps the most important and decisive attack (except that of the Prussian Guard on 10 November) made against the 1st Corps during the whole of its arduous experiences in the neighbourhood of Ypres'.

The Brigade Commander of 1st Guards Brigade, Brigadier-General Charles FitzClarence, one of the heroes of the First Battle of Ypres, played a crucial role at Gheluvelt by ordering the Worcesters' counter-attack there on 31 October. A veteran of the siege of Mafeking, where he had been awarded the VC, he was now 49 years of age and well accustomed to leading from the front. Charles FitzClarence was killed on 12 November, and his name now appears on the Menin Gate Memorial to the Missing in Ypres.

Brigadier General Charles FitzClarence, vc

IRISH GUARDS

Charles FitzClarence was an Irishman who had done most his active soldiering before the turn of the 20th century. Born in 1865, he joined the Royal Fusiliers at the age of 21, but ill-health kept him from the front line until 1899 when, in South Africa, he served with Robert Baden-Powell and, at the Siege of Mafeking, was awarded the VC. Commanding inexperienced soldiers while surrounded and outnumbered by the Boers, he led a night attack across open ground onto the enemy's trenches, killing four men with his sword. At Mafeking, FitzClarence had demonstrated coolness and courage, exceptional leadership skills, and a fine tactical eye, the perfect example of a Victorian hero, with a reputation as 'The Demon' that was to follow him for the remainder of his career.

In 1900 FitzClarence transferred to the Irish Guards, and in August 1914 was posted to command a brigade in the Curragh. Offering to lead 1st Irish Guards when the Commanding Officer, George Morris, was killed on 1 September 1914, instead he was posted to command 1st Guards Brigade, which had taken heavy casualties and was now dug in on the Aisne.

FitzClarence was no stranger to trench warfare, and in early October he ordered the first British trench raid of the war because 'I considered it a necessary duty to attack them'. Following the successful attack onto 'Fish Hook Trench' by 1st Coldstream, FitzClarence requested supplies of rifle grenades, sandbags, and steel plates, all items that were to become standard issue for trench warfare.

In mid-October the Brigade moved to Ypres where, on 19 October, the Germans launched massive infantry attacks supported by heavy artillery. It was a new kind of warfare, a shattering experience for the BEF, with attacks and counter-attacks along shallow trenches. In this kind of battle, for which most officers and soldiers alike had little training, FitzClarence was the ideal leader. He was always close to the front line, darting around, directing and leading his troops in one of the most confusing and fluid battles of the war.

The key moment came when FitzClarence was ordered to hold the eastern approaches to Gheluvelt, astride the Menin Road and less than 5 miles from Ypres. On 29 October the Germans attacked, with the Guards taking heavy casualties. Somehow, the line was held, but the real crisis came on 31 October, when the Germans managed to capture the village. For the British, this was the most critical event of the war so far and later described by Sir John French as the worst moment of his entire life.

With two divisional commanders incapacitated by shellfire, FitzClarence was now the only senior commander on the ground and, without any orders, he quickly decided upon an immediate counter-attack. He knew that the 2nd Worcesters, from another division, could be made available in an emergency, but the Worcesters had not been told. Patiently, FitzClarence carefully explained the situation to the Commanding Officer, and then gave his orders 'To advance without delay and deliver a counter-attack with the outmost vigour against the enemy'. The

Above: *Brigadier General Charles FitzClarence VC on the Aisne, September 1914 (second from right).*

Worcesters, a force of 8 officers and 370 men, were guided into position some 1,200 yards from the village by one of FitzClarence's staff officers, Captain Andrew 'Bulgy' Thorne, and then began their attack at around 2pm. The Germans were caught by surprise and, linking up with the South Wales Borderers, they drove the enemy from the village with their bayonets and at point-blank range. The counter-attack had been successful, though there was no breakthrough. The real heroes were the infantrymen with their rifles and bayonets, but Charles FitzClarence had played a crucial role on a day when the British came close to losing the war.

In the early hours of 12 November 1914, following hard fighting the previous day, Charles FitzClarence was killed by a single stray bullet close to Polygon Wood. He was on a trench raid, not something that brigade commanders normally did, but FitzClarence wanted to be there, to lead the Irish Guards, but also because manpower was short and he knew how to find the German trench. Somewhere in the column, a soldier had carelessly fired a round into the air, prompting more firing further forward. FitzClarence halted the advance, went forward to investigate, and then somewhere in the darkness was shot by a German. With FitzClarence now dead, there seemed little point in continuing the raid. 'Ma' Jeffreys, leading the Grenadiers, later wrote that without him 'we hadn't a chance of success'.

FitzClarence's body was found and buried but then lost, and so his name is recorded on the Menin Gate, at the far end of that road that he had defended so tenaciously in October and November 1914. Years later, as the most senior officer named on the memorial, he became known by veterans as 'GOC Menin Gate'.

'Bulgy' Thorne and Adolf Hitler

Andrew 'Bulgy' Thorne was commissioned into the Grenadier Guards in 1904 and by October 1914 was a staff officer serving on the Ypres Salient. By the end of the war, having commanded 3rd Battalion Grenadier Guards, he was a temporary brigadier general, aged 33, in command of a division before reverting to his substantive rank of major just a few weeks later.

In April 1932 Thorne became military attaché in Berlin in the rank of colonel, at a time when the Nazis were not yet in power but growing in strength. He arrived in Germany with an open mind, a respect for his former enemy, and a love for German music and opera. With the policy of non-fraternisation now rescinded, he and his wife Margaret were soon active on the diplomatic circuit, giving cocktail and dinner parties. In these turbulent times in Germany, the Thornes found themselves obliged to entertain some of the Nazi leaders such as Ernst Röhm and Hermann Goering, and they were still in Berlin in January 1933 when Hitler became Chancellor.

In 1934, learning that Thorne had been studying the Great War in the German war archives, Hitler asked to see him, and on 10 June they met. As Bulgy recounted to his son Peter: 'I was v. highly honoured . . . and had a 33 min. interview with the Führer, which was most awfully interesting and at which he was most charming. He discussed particularly the fighting at Gheluvelt in 1914 where he had his baptism of fire'. Thorne recounted to a Norwegian journalist 35 years later: 'For a long time we stood over the map exchanging reminiscences over

Above: *General von Schleicher, German Defence Minister (right), talking to Colonel Andrew Thorne, British Military Attaché (left). Military manoeuvres in Germany, 1932.*

the area where the fighting had taken place, the road along which the Germans attacked, the various fields and hills. Hitler was delighted and stressed that it was not pale faced staff officers but the ordinary front-line soldiers who could understand war. I tactfully refrained from telling him that I had actually been a staff officer at the time'. But it was clear to them both that they had been at Gheluvelt, not far from each other, and close to the crossroads where the fighting had taken place.

Despite Hitler's charm at this meeting, Thorne had no illusions about the dangers of Nazism and the growing threat to Britain and her allies. He continued to observe on and report all that he could see of the growing strength of the German army. He identified evidence of mechanisation, the gearing up of German car manufacturers to build tanks, and predicted that Germany would be ready for a highly mobile war within five years. The postscript in one of his reports was prescient: 'the whole tradition of the army is not to oppose the popular will and for the moment, and probably for some time, there will be no revulsion of feeling towards Hitler'.

Before leaving Berlin in the spring of 1935, Thorne reported the Germans' interest in the idea of a long-range rocket, and in his final report he recounted a meeting with General von Reichenau who spoke of plans to evacuate the Russian population eastwards and to leave Poland empty to allow the German population more living space. Reichenau hinted that Britain should allow Germany a free hand in Europe, and in return the Germans would not interfere with Britain's interests elsewhere. Although the report provoked some consternation back home, a passing comment by a German general was perhaps too easy to ignore.

Hitler respected this thoroughly professional British officer when they met in 1934, and it probably came as no surprise to him when Thorne was appointed General Officer Commanding-in-Chief Scottish Command in 1941, although for Thorne the appointment was something of a disappointment. What Hitler would not have known is that an important part of the job was to be responsible for the 'Fortitude North' deception plan designed to fool the Germans about an Allied invasion of Norway in 1944. Given Hitler's respect for Thorne, this could only have added credence to the deception.

There is a final footnote to the story. General Sir Andrew Thorne became Commander-in-Chief Allied Land Forces Norway in January 1945 and, just a few months later, the Führerbunker was searched following the liberation of Berlin. Among the charred remains of papers was a German translation of Bulgy Thorne's article about Gheluvelt 1914, published in the 1932 summer edition of the *Household Brigade Magazine*. It is an intriguing thought: was Hitler rereading this article in the bunker as the Third Reich collapsed around him? Perhaps the memory of two soldiers recounting a battle on a crossroads in Flanders over 30 years earlier had offered a very brief diversion during those last few days of Hitler's life?

Above: *Adolf Hitler (seated right) during his service with the Bavarian Reserve Infantry Regiment 16.*

ZANDVOORDE

On 20 October, the Household Cavalry occupied rough
trenches at Zandvoorde, described graphically by
Corporal of Horse Lloyd:

> there was no continuous line, the trenches were
> a series of holes, for all the world like large graves,
> not connected and running zig zag across the hillside.
> At the point where we struck [when approaching],
> each trench was chock full of men who absolutely
> refused to admit us. Once in a trench it was very
> hard to move without being shelled or sniped at, and
> rations could only be delivered at night, though the
> men would creep out to make tea at quiet intervals.

Right: *Field artillery battery of 2nd Division in position
in the open near Zandvoorde, 30 October 1914.*

Opposite: Jäger battalions.

Right: *Captain Stewart Menzies (2nd from right), 2nd Life Guards. In 1915 Menzies became an intelligence officer at GHQ and in 1919 transferred to MI1c, later the Secret Intelligence Service, or MI6. In 1939, just after the outbreak of the Second World War, he became 'C', the head of MI6.*

Shortly before 7am, 260 German guns began to bombard the front line, and about 30 minutes later three Jäger battalions attacked. The combination of artillery and the infantry assault was devastating, and very quickly these inadequate trenches were being overrun. Captain Stewart Menzies, Adjutant of 2nd Life Guards, described the battle:

> Practically nothing is known of what occurred as the two squadrons and the machine guns of the Blues completely disappeared, and only very few survivors were taken prisoner, and on their return at the end of the war they were unable, I understand, to throw much light on the attack. I can only conclude that the squadrons were cut off owing to their somewhat forward position and were ultimately all killed, though it is remarkable that there should have been so few taken prisoners. Some of the trenches were very primitive, and I remember one that was too deep to allow the occupants to see over the top, and they would hardly be in a position to offer any effective resistance. But on the other hand other trenches were quite well sited and the whole incident has always struck me as one of the most remarkable occurrences of the war. I fear that one must assume that the Germans behaved in an ultra Hunlike manner and gave no quarter.

Field Marshal Haig recalled the action after the war:

> They were in narrow trenches on the forward slopes before us in full sight of the enemy. Their trenches were soon blown in and at 8am after one and a quarter hours bombardment the whole of the 39th German Infantry Division and three battalions of Jägers attacked their shattered position. The time had come to slip away and orders were issued for the retirement to the second line; but the greater part of two squadrons of Life Guards on the left and the Royal Horse Guards machine guns could not get away and were cut off and died to a man, except for a few wounded prisoners.

The following day, on 31 October, the Composite Regiment was attacked in its trenches between Wytschaete and Messines. The Commanding Officer, Lieutenant Colonel Edwin Cook, had been wounded earlier, Lord Cavendish was dead and command had now passed to Major the Viscount Crichton. The Germans attacked in the moonlight, the Household Cavalry held the line, and on two occasions regained positions they had earlier lost. But eventually the Germans prevailed with their much greater strength, and the Composite Regiment was forced back.

Private James MacKenzie, VC

SCOTS GUARDS

James MacKenzie was born in 1889, at West Glen, near Dumfries. After leaving school, he worked on a number of farms before moving to Maxwelltown to become a joiner. He enlisted in the Scots Guards in early 1912, stating his age to be 22 when he was actually 27. Over the next two years he served mostly at Caterham and Aldershot, was posted absent, for which he received a punishment of two days 'confined to barracks', and was given a similar punishment of three days for firing from the wrong parapet on the Pirbright Ranges.

On 5 October 1914, James MacKenzie embarked with the 2nd Battalion for France. On 18 December 1914, the Scots Guards took part in a two-day action on the Sailly–Fromelles Road where there were many casualties to intensive German machine-gun fire during an attack on enemy trenches. This was part of a fierce hand-to-hand two-day action in which he won the VC for rescuing a severely wounded comrade under heavy fire. His citation reads: 'For conspicuous bravery at Rouges Bancs on the 19th December 1914, in rescuing a severely wounded man from in front of the German trenches, under a very heavy fire and after a stretcher-bearer party had been compelled to abandon the attempt. Private Mackenzie was subsequently killed on that day whilst in the performance of a similar act of gallant conduct'.

One of MacKenzie's comrades later wrote: 'He was returning to the trenches along with me and another stretcher-bearer when it occurred. We had only two or three cases that morning, so the last one was taken by us three. After we took the wounded soldier to hospital we returned to see if there were any more. There was a very dangerous place to pass. I went first, followed by another, then James came behind, which caused his death. He was shot in the heart by a sniper, and only lived five minutes'.

James MacKenzie has no known grave, and his name appears on the Ploegsteert Memorial to the Missing in Belgium.

Crichton was killed that day and, when the roll was called on 1 November, only 63 answered their name. It was to be the last action for the Composite Regiment; it was soon disbanded and the survivors re-joined their parent regiments.

On 6 November, the 7th Cavalry Brigade (1st and 2nd Life Guards and the Royal Horse Guards) was ordered into action to strengthen the line at Klein Zillebeke, the boundary between the French troops and the 4th Guards Brigade. Here, just to the north-east of the Comines Canal, the French had been pushed back by a determined German attack supported by intense artillery fire. Two Chasseur battalions panicked, a mile of the front line lay open, and the enemy thrust

itself into the gap. A company of Irish Guards, now with a dangerously exposed flank, was completely destroyed while another was forced to pull back. Now it was the turn of the 'Fire Brigade', as 7th Cavalry Brigade had come to be known. Deploying swiftly across the front on their horses, the Household Cavalry dismounted and charged on foot, driving the Germans back 'at the point of the bayonet'. Among those killed was Lieutenant the Honourable Reginald Wyndham who had served with the 17th Lancers in the South African War, retired from the Army in 1903, and was now back in the Army, aged 38.

It had been a quieter time for the 1st (Royal) Dragoons, but they had also taken casualties. On 17 November, Julian Grenfell jumped into what appeared to be an empty trench, but soon found a German soldier and shot him. Realising it might not be safe to leave, he waited and then saw a group of Germans approaching. He shot the officer and got back to the Royals' trenches

by a 'galloping crawl' in time to deliver a warning of the impending German attack. He was later awarded a Distinguished Service Order (DSO).

The First Battle of Ypres ended on 22 November as the cold weather began to take its grip on the stark landscape. Crucially, the Allies had held the line along what became known as the Ypres Salient, while the Germans' attempt to get to the sea was over for the time being. The Guards regiments that fought at the First Battle of Ypres had been all but destroyed, and there was now a stark realisation both here and back home that this war would not be won easily or quickly. For example, following the attacks on 10 and 11 November, 2nd Grenadiers had been reduced to just 3 officers and 74 men, struggling on in the line until the drafts of older reservists began arriving in late November and early December.

Lieutenant the Honourable Reginald Wyndham

THE LIFE GUARDS

The Honourable Reginald Wyndham, born in 1875, served with the 17th Lancers from 1896 to 1903. In August 1914, aged 38, he was commissioned into the Lincolnshire Yeomanry, then transferred to The Life Guards. His father had served in the regiment, and his two younger brothers, Edward and Humphrey ('Humpty' to both his family and his soldiers) were serving officers and both later commanded The Life Guards.

Corporal of Horse Robert Lloyd recalled Reggie Wyndham's arrival at Knightsbridge Barracks: 'an officer who had come back from retirement dressed in a rig-out which was a sight of the gods. His khaki jacket fitted him where it touched him; his riding pants were of coarse material, baggy, and reminiscent of knickerbockers at the knees. He wore in addition a pair of thick greased hob-nailed boots, rough puttees, and a cap from which the wire had been removed and which looked as if it had been slept on. On his Sam Browne belt was a stout iron hook from which dangled a pair of hedging-and-ditching gloves. Before he had advanced ten paces inside the barrack gate he was unanimously christened "Sinbad the Sailor" . . . . In spite of his weird uniform, Sinbad was a fine soldier and gentleman. When someone chipped him about his turnout, I heard him reply: "My dear sir, you'll all be dressed like this, or worse, before Christmas".'

Reggie began his diary on 5 October 1914, the day he departed from Ludgershall Camp in Hampshire en route to Southampton Docks. From then on he made daily entries until 4 November, two days before he was killed at Klein Zillebeke, near Ypres.

Friday 30th October. 'In the morning they all attacked us. They shelled us hard, and one of the first shells buried Dawes all except his head, and also buried my belt, pillow, glasses and haversack. Then their infantry attacked. We knocked a good few over, but the Maxim on our right ran out of ammunition, and one trench on our right was driven in. We kept on firmly until our ammunition was finished. The spare box of ammunition was buried by the shell which buried Dawes. In the end we had no more ammunition, and they began to enfilade us from our right. Had to order Sergeant Arthurs to retire from the right hand trench, and then ordered my troop to retire. Previous to this had dug Dawes out with my hands. Before we started to retire, Corp. Brooks had been slightly hit in two places. We ran back to the farm. The Maxim killed Sergeant Arthurs. Then after finding Clowes had left the farm, I went on, and found Dawes and Brooks. Dawes was slightly hit. We found Bussey badly wounded, but could not move him. We picked up a man of Arthurs' troop and helped him along till he dropped dead. Then when we reached the X roads where Levigne was buried, Dawes had his leg broken by the shell fire. The shells had been bursting just over us all the way. Had to leave Dawes lying where he was. Then met Humphrey, who told me the order to retire had been signalled to me. Then met General Kavanagh [commanding 7th Brigade] who told me that he wished me to retire. Then set to work to find the men. Found most of them when we got back to the horses. As we retired down the road, the Germans shelled it, and Charlie Fitzmaurice was killed. Then found that my troop of twenty had 9 killed and wounded, and there were only 7 left of Arthurs' troop of 26 men. We camped tonight in Verbranden Moues. As we had no blankets since Sunday night, it was a blessing to get a night of rest. Algy joined us near the camping ground where the

Right: *The memorial to Reginald Wyndham in the churchyard at Zillebeke records that he is known to have been buried somewhere nearby, his actual burial place having been lost in the war damage of the following four years.*

horses were, and he had only been shelled this morning slightly. Althorp had been hit by a spent bullet in the thigh. The Guards took up the defence of our front, and a brigade under Bulkeley-Johnson came to our assistance. Pickles Lambton was killed in the trenches last night, and Hugh Grosvenor and all his squadron bar Jerry Ward and a few men are missing. They say this is the biggest battle of the whole war, and our casualties are 18,000 which is a greater list than Mons.'

Reggie Wyndham was killed on 6 November while leading his men in a spirited dismounted bayonet charge to recover trenches lost earlier that day. After darkness fell that night, two troopers from the machine-gun section ventured out with two horses and a half-limber, found Reggie's body and brought him back to the nearby cemetery beside the church at Zillebeke, where he still lies.

1ST BATTALION
WELSH GUARDS 1915

The early months of 1915 gave the Guards an opportunity to develop their new trench warfare skills. The routine was a steady one while it lasted, relying on strict discipline, vigilance among the sentries, particularly at night when there were double sentries on duty, the cleaning of equipment, and regular inspections and visits by commanding officers and company officers. When not on duty in the trenches, there were route marches, range firing, and lessons on new techniques. Reservists continued to arrive, a few luxuries from England began to appear, and for the first time there was an opportunity for some home leave.

'Ma' Jeffreys, now in the rank of lieutenant colonel and commanding 2nd Grenadiers, described the routine when the battalion was in the trenches:

> We stand to an hour before daybreak until it is quite light. Then if all is quiet, everybody gets on to cleaning selves, arms, equipment, trenches and day sentries (single and fewer posts) are posted. We have very strict orders for sentries and drop heavily on the slightest slackness. They have to be constantly looking out – in the front line through periscopes – and are not allowed to sit down, talk to other men, smoke or allow any distraction. At night a double sentry on each post, no Balaclava helmet over their ears. All men wear equipment and rifles. All ammunition, other than in men's pouches, is to be kept in boxes and not left loose or in bandoliers. We try to keep everybody soldierlike and clean and tidy as possible and don't allow anyone to degenerate into a scallywag. We, CO and 2i/c, make regular rounds by day and night and company officers go round constantly.

Although there were no large-scale offensives during those early months of 1915, there was plenty of activity in the form of aggressive patrolling,

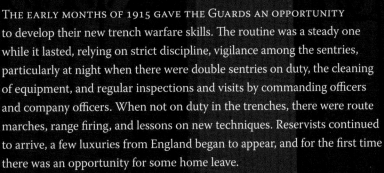

Formation of the 1st Battalion Welsh Guards, White City, Shepherd's Bush, March 1915. Some of the men transferred from other Guards Regiments.

Above: *Lieutenant Sir Edward Hamilton Westrow Hulse and four men of 2nd Battalion, Scots Guards with whom he raided a trench near Sailly-sur-la-Lys on the night of 27 November 1914. Sir Edward was killed in attack on the Moulin du Pietre near Neuve Chapelle on 12 March 1915.*

Left: *Coldstream Guards in a trench, April 1915.*

days later, in the early hours of 1 February, the Germans rushed the front-line trenches of 2nd Coldstream. Already holding an extended stretch of the line, the Coldstream were reinforced by 1st Irish Guards for the counter-attack. It was a close-run battle, but the Guards managed to regain and hold the line. A ten-minute barrage of rifle fire, so intense that the Germans believed they were being engaged by machine guns, helped to turn the battle, and it was here that Lance Corporal Michael O'Leary, Irish Guards, won his VC.

local skirmishing and the occasional clash. One such engagement came on 25 January when 1st Coldstream suffered 200 casualties in a German attack that was preceded by the blowing of four large mines. A few

NEUVE CHAPELLE

The Battle of Neuve Chapelle in March 1915 was the first major British attack of the war. On an open, flat and muddy battleground, and with the Germans on slightly higher ground along Aubers Ridge, the offensive began on the morning of 10 March with a short but intensive artillery bombardment. The initial infantry attack, led by the Indians, was a success. By nightfall Neuve Chapelle had been taken, but the Germans now quickly reinforced their second line.

1st Grenadiers attacked the following morning, advancing from trenches captured the previous day. But it was soon apparent that much of the information given to the battalion prior to the attack was incorrect, with most of the known landmarks having been obliterated. Furthermore, the Germans were still holding part of their old line and so the Grenadiers found themselves turning around to attack the enemy behind them. It was an impossible and highly confused situation, compounded by 'a murderous enfilade fire from the German machine-guns on [the Grenadiers'] left front, which very much puzzled the men, who imagined the enemy to be straight in front of them'. Somehow, despite heavy losses, they held their positions, later retiring to some reserve trenches,

hearing, as they moved back, 'the piteous cries of the wounded and dying, who asked not to be trodden on'.

On 12 March, the Grenadiers advanced again, in support of 2nd Scots Guards. There followed a most confusing few hours during which some of the Guards were sent in the wrong direction and part of the attack was launched too early. But somehow, through a 'labyrinth of trenches' the Guards found their assigned positions, ready for the advance. It was about this time that the Grenadiers' Commanding Officer, Lieutenant Colonel Lawrence Fisher Rowe, was hit by a bullet in the head and killed.

The Scots Guards and Border Regiment now conducted their main attack without any British artillery support, and it was during this phase that two VCs were won by Grenadiers: Private Edward Barber, who captured over 100 Germans before being shot by a sniper; and Lance Corporal Wilfred Fuller, who captured a party of enemy attempting to escape along a communication trench.

A few days after the battle, Lieutenant Alan Swinton, Scots Guards, wrote:

We fell in at 4.30 am, and started marching round to a point given to me the night before. We had to go along

Left: *Captain the Honourable H. R. L. Alexander, Irish Guards (later to become Field Marshal Earl Alexander of Tunis), in the trenches at Laventie in 1915.*

Private Edward Barber, VC
GRENADIER GUARDS

Edward Barber was born in Tring in 1893, and worked as a bricklayer's labourer before joining the Grenadier Guards in 1911. He was due to be transferred to the Reserve when war broke out, but instead was soon on his way to France with the 1st Battalion. Edward Barber was awarded his VC for his action at Neuve Chapelle on 12 March 1915. His citation was published on 19 February: 'For most conspicuous bravery . . . . he ran speedily in front of the grenade company to which he belonged, and threw bombs on the enemy with such effect that a very great number of them at once surrendered. When the grenade party reached Private Barber they found him quite alone and unsupported, with the enemy surrendering all about him'.

Lance Corporal Wilfred Fuller, also awarded a VC on that day, found Edward Barber's body and also a letter in his pocket addressed to a cousin living at Slough, to whom he wrote 'while doing his duty he was picked off by a German sniper. The bullet penetrated his brain, death being instantaneous . . . . Your cousin feared nothing and he was the finest man we had, both in wit and courage'. Edward Barber's body was never recovered, and he was later posted as presumed dead. His mother was presented with her son's medal by King George V. 'Of course, we are very proud' she told a journalist, 'but I can't bear to lose my boy. What is the Victoria Cross to the loss of my son?'

a typical French road, straight with trees on each side . . . . Several trees had fallen across the road, shrapnel was bursting over it, it ran parallel to our lines, so there was a cross fire over it, also the Huns were using trench mortars, and chucking bombs by them on and over the road; how we got along I don't know, but no one was hit. Anyway, I got down to our meeting point and found George; we lay down, but had not been there more than five minutes, when they began to shell like the devil. The only thing we could do was to

Continued on page 68.

64

Lance Corporal Wilfred Fuller, VC

GRENADIER GUARDS

Wilfred Fuller was born in East Kirkby in 1893, and after leaving school worked at a local colliery where his father was manager. He joined the Grenadier Guards in 1911, and in October 1914 went with the 1st Battalion to France.

Wilfred Fuller was awarded the VC for his action at Neuve Chapelle on 12 March 1915. His citation was published on 19 February: 'For most conspicuous bravery . . . . Seeing a party of the enemy endeavouring to escape along a communication trench, he ran towards them and killed the leading man with a bomb; the remainder (nearly 50) finding no means of evading his bombs, surrendered to him. Lance Corporal Fuller was quite alone at the time'. He received his medal from the King, and when he visited his home town, the mayor gave an address in the town square and presented him with a gold watch. In his reply, Fuller said 'I only did my duty. I am going out again and I don't mind dying for my country'.

Wilfred Fuller did not return to the front, and because of his wounds was discharged as medically unfit in 1916. At first, he did not find it easy to get work, but he then joined the Somerset police, with whom he served until retiring in 1939, due to ill health. He died in 1947.

Left: *Lance Corporal Fuller received his VC from King George V at Buckingham Palace on 4 June 1915. In this photograph, taken on 30 September 1915 at No. 3 Base Hospital, Sheffield, the King is presenting Lance Corporal Fuller with the Russian Order of St George.*

Lance Corporal Michael O'Leary, VC

IRISH GUARDS

Michael O'Leary was born in County Cork in 1888, and later worked on his father's farm before joining the navy in 1909. Discharged as unfit the following year, within three months he had joined the Irish Guards where he stayed until transferred to the Reserve in 1913. He then went to Canada, serving with the Royal North-West Mounted Police in Saskatchewan. On the outbreak of war he re-joined the Irish Guards in England, and by November 1914 was in France. He was promoted to Lance Corporal in early 1915, and on 1 February took part in a counter-attack on the Cuinchy sector to recover trenches lost earlier that morning. As part of a small party ordered forward to support the Coldstream Guards, he ran out in front of his comrades, climbed a railway embankment, and fired at an enemy machine-gun post, killing its crew. Another 60 yards on he encountered a second machine gun, which he also attacked, killing three Germans and taking two prisoners who did not know that he had now run out of ammunition. Bringing his prisoners back to the British front line, and in the words of Company Quartermaster Sergeant Lowry, he was 'as cool as if he had been for a walk in the park'.

Although the Guards had taken heavy casualties, the counter-attack had been successful, largely due to O'Leary's actions which resulted in not only the retaking of lost ground but the gaining of ground that led to the Germans pulling back further. O'Leary was promoted in the field to sergeant, and on 18 February his citation was published in the *London Gazette*: 'For conspicuous bravery at Cuinchy on the 1st February, 1915. When forming one of the storming party which advanced against the enemy's barricades he rushed to the front and himself killed five Germans who were holding the first barricade, after which he attacked a second barricade about 60 yards further on, which he captured, after killing three of the enemy and making prisoners of two more. Lance Corporal O'Leary thus practically captured the enemy's position by himself, and prevented the rest of the attacking party from being fired upon'.

O'Leary became a celebrity back home, where he was soon part of a recruiting campaign which included Ireland where fewer men had joined up. Songs and poems were written about him, and George Bernard Shaw wrote a one-act play, *O'Flaherty V.C.*, inspired by his story. O'Leary's VC was the first for Ireland and the Irish Guards, and he became a national hero. For a while the Irish Guards were 'O'Leary's Lads', and 11 July became 'O'Leary Day'. One poster encouraged Irishmen to follow his example: 'An Irish Hero! 1 Irishman defeats 10 Germans. Have you no wish to emulate the splendid bravery of your fellow countryman[?]' His parents were interviewed by local reporters – with his father recorded as saying 'I am surprised he didn't do more. I often laid out 20 men myself with a stick coming from Macroom Fair, and it is a bad trial of Mick that he could kill only eight, and he having a rifle and bayonet'.

Michael O'Leary was later commissioned in the Connaught Rangers and after the war became an inspector in the Ontario provincial police, where he ended up in court twice for smuggling liquor and then an alien across the border. The Canadians were reluctant to deport a war hero, and so he was quietly allowed to leave. He served in the Pioneer Corps during the Second World War, retiring as a major. He later became a building contractor in London, where he died in 1961.

The story of Michael O'Leary conformed to some of the well-known Irish stereotypes. He had come a long way from farm-boy to the holder of a VC and later a commission in the British Army. He was a colourful character and a bit of a rogue, but above all, had displayed courage on that day in 1915, and by his actions almost certainly saved the lives of others.

Above: *An illustration celebrating O'Leary's valiant action.*

Left: *'Sergeant Mike O'Leary, V.C.'; sheet music published in 1915.*

try to get the battalion into the trenches from which we were to make our attack, so George and I led on, hoping that the men would follow, as the distance was some 500 yards. The company got terribly strung out; several were hit, and the shells were bursting like the devil. You cannot imagine anything worse than being shelled in the dark, it is much worse than in daylight. Eventually we got to the place with about six men, the remainder being strung out behind. Anyway, we got under cover and sat there till daylight.

The attack was due to begin at 8am, but had been delayed due to fog. The battalion was now ready:

We scrambled out into the open alongside the trench, ready to start off . . . [and] at 10.30 we got up and advanced; we were greeted at once by rapid rifle and

machine-gun fire. I honestly wouldn't have believed it possible that anything could have lived in that fire; lots were hit . . . . but I ran on until I found a trench . . . 2 feet deep and 2 feet wide; into this I dropped and started to dig myself in with my bayonet; here I stayed until 1.30. In the meantime we learnt that we had attacked too early; that orderlies had been sent [out to pass the message] postponing the attack till 12.30, because the artillery could not see to bombard; both these orderlies had been killed, so we had never got the message, and we had attacked too early; hence the fire against us. Anyway, at noon the bombardment began, we of course were all lying flat in our scrapes, as the Huns were shooting all the time. I never heard such a noise as this bombardment in my life, one continuous roar the whole time. Soon it was passed along that the Huns were putting up white flags. I looked up and saw that they were coming out of their trenches on the left; at that moment Pip Warner got up and shouted to me to come on, so I followed him with about 4 men, and we assisted taking in the prisoners – some 500–600. We then went on . . . firing at the retreating Huns. I was then sent back for reinforcements, and, having seen those all off, found I could not get back, as the fire was too heavy from the right, so I had to sit in the trench till dark. Later on in the night we were withdrawn, cold and weary, and this ends my experience in the Battle of Neuve Chapelle.

The battle ended in stalemate with only minor tactical gains. The Germans had all the advantages where just one machine gun, firing across a featureless battlefield, could cause havoc. At Neuve Chapelle, the Grenadiers had 16 officers killed, and 325 soldiers killed or wounded; while 2nd Scots Guards had lost a total of 23 killed, 85 missing, and 182 wounded.

Left: *Lieutenant Alan Swinton, Scots Guards.*

Edward Cazalet, Welsh Guards

A BRIEF LIFE

Edward Cazalet was born in 1894, and after leaving school went to Hanover to learn German with a view to joining the Diplomatic Service. He was in Berlin at the outbreak of war, and, with English banknotes no longer accepted, managed to return home by train with the help of some gold sovereigns given to him by the Berlin correspondent of *The Times*. He joined the Officer Training Corps at Cambridge, and in 1915 was commissioned in the Buffs, transferring to the Welsh Guards in the same year. In 1916, he was assigned to guard Sir Roger Casement, the traitor and Irish patriot, in the Tower of London, shortly before Casement was taken to Pentonville to be hanged on 3 August 1916. Cazalet found him to have a 'charming manner and beautiful voice, a nicer person I have seldom met, his ideals and ambitions for the world's general happiness and improvement couldn't be better. It seems a terrible pity that he should have committed this last monstrous deed of trying to stir up Ireland while England was at war'.

Before he left for France in July 1916, Edward wrote to his mother saying he had a horror of killing people; the idea of shooting even a German made him feel sick. Once on the front line, he wrote to his younger brother Victor, serving with the Household Battalion, describing life in the trenches: 'I am in the most smelly of trenches, the result of a large number of bodies being buried close by. The rats are quite innumerable'. On 18 August 1916 he found himself 'In a very small dugout similar I should imagine to the Black Hole of Calcutta. This part is rather smelly, as not long ago the enemy began shelling our line. The

gas cylinders were broken and a very large number of our men were gassed. The numbers were so large that the bodies were not recorded, so it is not uncommon to come across the arm or leg of these unhappy soldiers'.

Edward Cazalet was killed on 10 September 1916 at the Battle of Ginchy, during the Somme offensive. His soldier-servant, Private Williams, later wrote to his mother, Molly Cazalet: 'I can assure you that everything that could be done for Mr Cazalet was done, but it was all in vain and he was killed almost instantaneously. I also did what he wanted to be done if anything should happen to him as he was talking to me two or three days before he went into action. So he was brought down the line about ten miles where Mr Cazalet and his great friend, Mr Wernher are lying together'.

Right: *Mrs Cazalet with Edward and Victor, March 1916.*

Julian Grenfell
1ST (ROYAL) DRAGOONS

Julian Grenfell was born in London in 1888, and from his early days at school wrote poems and later articles for magazines such as *Vanity Fair*. At Oxford, he enjoyed academic life and all outdoor pursuits, including hunting, and he excelled as a sportsman. As one of his contemporaries commented: 'He rowed, he hunted; and he read, and he roared with laughter, and he cracked his whip in the quad all night; he bought greyhounds, boxed all the local champions; [wrote] poetry . . . and charmed everybody'.

Grenfell joined the 1st (Royal) Dragoons in 1910, serving first in India and then South Africa. He clearly enjoyed the active military life, while also continuing to be creative, writing poems, articles, and plays for his soldiers to perform. But sooner or later, he would have tired of peacetime soldiering had the war not come in 1914. Grenfell was soon in France, where he seemed to enjoy himself from the outset. 'I adore war', he wrote, 'It's like a big picnic, without the objectivelessness of a picnic. I've never been so well or so happy'.

Julian Grenfell was in his element in those early confusing days, and soon gained a reputation for his devil-may-care style of courage. In November 1914, he was awarded the DSO for conducting a daring 'individual reconnaissance', in which he stalked German snipers, killing them at close range. He was a brave and a natural risk-taker, and it was perhaps inevitable that his luck would not hold out indefinitely. He was wounded by splinters in his head on 13 May

1915, near Ypres, and died two weeks later in hospital in Boulogne, with his parents and sister, a Red Cross nurse, at his bedside.

Julian Grenfell is now remembered particularly for his poem 'Into Battle', which he had written a few weeks earlier as his regiment waited for the next big battle to begin. It appeared in *The Times* in the same edition that announced his death.

'Into Battle'
by Julian Grenfell

The naked earth is warm with spring,
And with green grass and bursting trees
Leans to the sun's gaze glorying,
And quivers in the sunny breeze;
And life is colour and warmth and light,
And a striving evermore for these;
And he is dead who will not fight;
And who dies fighting has increase.

The fighting man shall from the sun
Take warmth, and life from the glowing earth;
Speed with the light-foot winds to run,
And with the trees to newer birth;
And find, when fighting shall be done,
Great rest and fullness after dearth.

All the bright company of Heaven
Hold him in their high comradeship,
The Dog-Star, and the Sisters Seven,
Orion's Belt and sworded hip.

The woodland trees that stand together,
They stand to him each one a friend;
They gently speak in the windy weather;
They guide to valley and ridge's end.

The kestrel hovering by day,
And the little owls that call by night,
Bid him be swift and keen as they,
As keen of ear, as swift of sight.

The blackbird sings to him, 'Brother, brother,
If this be the last song you shall sing,
Sing well, for you may not sing another;
Brother, sing.'

In dreary, doubtful, waiting hours,
Before the brazen frenzy starts,
The horses show him nobler powers;
O patient eyes, courageous hearts!

And when the burning moment breaks,
And all things else are out of mind,
And only Joy of Battle takes
Him by the throat, and makes him blind,

Through joy and blindness he shall know,
Not caring much to know, that still
Nor lead nor steel shall reach him, so
That it be not the Destined Will.
The thundering line of battle stands,
And in the air Death moan and sings;
But Day shall clasp him with strong hands,
And Night shall fold him in soft wings.

THE FORMATION OF THE WELSH GUARDS

On 6 February 1915, the Major General, Sir Francis Lloyd, met the Secretary of State for War, Lord Kitchener, and discussed King George V's wish that a regiment of Welsh Guards be formed. 'When do you wish them to be ready?' he asked Kitchener. 'Immediately' was the response. 'Very well, sir. They shall go on Guard on St David's Day.' The Royal Warrant was signed on 26 February, and three days later the battalion mounted its first King's Guard at Buckingham Palace, on 1 March: St David's Day. The Captain of the Guard was the Commanding Officer, Lieutenant Colonel William Murray-Threipland, formerly Grenadier Guards, and Lord Kitchener dined with him at St James's that evening. On 19 March, the leading company was given the title of 'Prince of Wales's Company', and just before departing for France on 17 August, the battalion received its first colours from the King.

Above: *Welsh Guards mounting their first King's Guard at Buckingham Palace on 1 March 1915, St David's Day.*

Above top: *Detachment of 1st Welsh Guards on arrival and in new uniform at Chelsea Barracks.*

Left: *William Scott-Kerr was born in 1866 and took the name Murray-Threipland in 1882 following his inheritance of the estates of his cousin. He was commissioned in Grenadier Guards in 1887, seeing action in the Sudan and the South African War. In 1915 he was appointed to command 1st Battalion Welsh Guards on its formation, leading them with distinction at the Battle of Loos, where he was awarded the DSO. In 1937 William became the Colonel of the Welsh Guards.*

FESTUBERT

The Battle of Festubert, the first night attack of the war, began just before midnight on 15 May 1915. It was to be a continuation of the earlier attempt to capture Aubers Ridge, an attritional battle in which success would rely on heavy artillery. The problem, however, was the shortage of guns and shells, compounded by much-improved German defences.

20th Brigade attacked at 3.15am on 16 May, with 2nd Scots Guards leading on the right and 1st Grenadiers supporting the Border Regiment on the left. The Scots Guards took their objective relatively easily, while the Border Regiment was held up by German machine guns. The Grenadiers, under heavy shellfire, were now ordered forward to protect the Scots Guards' open flank, a consequence of a spirited attack in which F Company had been completely surrounded. The two Guards' commanding officers, meeting to assess a situation described later as 'very obscure', now made a hasty plan. By early evening, in heavy rain, two Grenadier companies were occupying old German trenches on the left of the Scots Guards' forward positions, but in miserable conditions. Everyone was weary and wet, the wounded lay out in the open, and there was every prospect of more action to follow. Among the Scots Guards, all of F Company and a platoon of Left Flank were missing, although 37 survivors made it back that night; Right Flank could only muster 30 men; and of the 16 officers that had gone forward that day, 6 remained.

Early on 17 May the Guards pushed on another 400 yards in conditions of torrential rain and knee-deep mud. Then, unexpectedly, 4th Guards Brigade appeared to the right of 1st Grenadiers, a memorable moment as they came forward 'in artillery formation, under a hail of shells and bullets'. By chance, two Grenadier

Above: *Chocolat Menier Corner, Rue du Bois. Princes Road to the right, by which Scots Guards left the trenches after the Battle of Festubert.*

battalions were now side by side for a short time before 20th Brigade was relieved that evening. They had done well. Despite constant counter-attacks, the positions along the line had all been held, but at a cost. The Scots Guards alone had suffered over 400 casualties, killed, wounded, or missing.

The battle was not yet over. 4th Guards Brigade, with 2nd Grenadiers, 1st Irish Guards and the 1st Hertfordshire Regiment (the 'Hertfordshire Guards'), went into action at 4.30pm on 18 May; 600 yards of open ground and water-filled ditches lay ahead. The first Grenadier platoon was literally mown down by machine-gun fire before it had covered 100 yards, and the next two literally 'melted away' before they could overtake the first. The Irish Guards, attacking on a wider front, suffered the same fate, as the Grenadiers on their left observed the 'gallant manner in which they brought up reinforcements . . . unfortunately with no success'. Further attacks were contemplated, but Lord Cavan, the Brigade Commander,

A Prince at the Front

The Prince of Wales was commissioned into the Grenadier Guards when war broke out and joined the King's Company despite being only 5ft 7in tall. Informed that he could not deploy overseas, he wrote to his Commanding Officer 'It was ghastly to see the Battalion all marched off. However the higher authorities won't let me go and so the matter must end . . . . I might get out on some staff, but I feel the firing line is the only thing that will satisfy me'. Two months later he wrote to a friend: 'It is terrible for me to sit here and see all my friends being killed or wounded on all sides'. Once the front line settled, he was allowed out to France where he served on the staff at General Headquarters. When told that he might get killed, his response was 'It doesn't matter if I am. I have four brothers'.

He then became assistant to Major Andrew 'Bulgy' Thorne, Grenadier Guards (in HQ 1st Division), who described him as 'Such a good fellow but extraordinarily young in every way but a most determined creature when he has made up his mind'. He managed to make visits to the front, and on one occasion narrowly escaped being hit by a shell. On a visit to the trenches at Givenchy in April 1915, he tried his hand at sniping, and the soldiers were certainly impressed: they ran a sweepstake for the empty bullet cases. In July 1915, he spent his first night in the trenches, afterwards writing to his father: 'My impressions that night were of close proximity to death, repugnance from the stink of unburied corpses'. Two months later he joined the staff of the newly formed Guards Division just prior to the Battle of Loos. One night he was given the task of directing traffic on a crossroads, standing deep in the mud. He later recorded his impressions of the Guards as they came up from the rear to take their place in the front line: 'they put on one of the finest exhibitions of discipline ever seen on any battlefield. Topping the flaming ridge, company by company in extended order, they moved into the attack down the shrapnel-raked hill before Loos as seemingly unconcerned as if training at Pirbright'. A few days later he and Lord Cavan had a lucky escape

when, on a tour of the front, they narrowly missed a burst of machine-gun fire. His driver was killed in the car parked 50 yards away, and the Prince later saw his body in the dressing station, 'he was hit in the heart and death must have been instantaneous . . . it's an absolute tragedy and I can't yet realise it's happened'.

In June 1916, the Prince of Wales was awarded the Military Cross, later writing to a friend that 'I do not feel I deserve it in the least. There are many gallant officers who should have MCs long before me'. But he did take some pleasure that it had been awarded to him for his service in the war and not merely for being the Prince of Wales.

After the war, in a speech he gave when he received the Freedom of the City of London, he described the part he played as 'a very insignificant one', but one that he never regretted. He was popular with veterans, and his admiration for the Guards never left him. 'The Guards Division was a great club' he wrote, 'and if tinged with snobbishness, it was the snobbishness of tradition, discipline, perfection, and sacrifice. They were the shock troops of the British Army; their prestige was purchased in blood'.

Left: *The Prince of Wales's rifle and ashplant walking stick.*

wisely decided to dig in and consolidate. Among those wounded was Lieutenant Colonel Wilfred Smith, the Commanding Officer of 2nd Grenadiers; he died on 19 May, the same day that 4th Guards Brigade was relieved in the front line. The village of Festubert was finally captured on 24 May, with the front line moving forward by less than 2 miles. The British had suffered some 16,600 casualties in five days of fighting.

On 15 July 1915, it was announced that His Majesty the King was 'graciously pleased to approve' the formation of two further battalions of Foot Guards: 4th Grenadier Guards and 2nd Irish Guards. Three days later, the formation took place. For the Irish Guards, there was an added significance because until that time there had been only one battalion and, as Rudyard Kipling says in the 2nd Battalion's history,

> Officers and men alike welcomed it, for it is less pleasing to be absorbed in drafts and driblets by an ever-hungry 1st Battalion in France than to be set apart for the sacrifice as a veritable Battalion on its own responsibility, with its traditions (they sprang up immediately) and its own esprit de corps.

On 6 August, the battalion paraded for its first route march, over 16 miles in the area around Warley Barracks, near Brentwood in Essex. It was a hot day, and the soldiers marched with their equipment, except for the 'Officer who had bethought him to fill his "full pack" with a full-blown air-cushion' and whose 'unlucky fraud betrayed him by bursting almost under the Adjutant's eye'. By the third week of August, the battalion was in France and, on 30 August, the two Irish Guards battalions met each other in the field for the first time. A month later they would be committed, as part of the newly formed Guards Division, at the Battle of Loos.

THE GUARDS DIVISION

The idea of the Guards Division had been Lord Kitchener's and it seems that once he had the King's approval, he went ahead with the arrangements without any discussion with the War Cabinet or the Commander-in-Chief of the BEF. Indeed, the first indication that Sir John French had was a letter from Kitchener in July 1915 telling him of his plans and the name of the first General Officer Commanding (GOC), the Earl of Cavan. Kitchener asked him 'whether you like this idea', but French could hardly have objected since the King had already been consulted. In any event French's position as Commander-in-Chief was becoming more strained. The Prime Minister, Herbert Asquith, had recently been in discussions about French's future and, just two weeks before Kitchener's letter, the King had concluded that French should go.

On 16 July, Kitchener told Major General Sir Francis Lloyd to prepare 3rd and 4th Grenadiers, 2nd Irish Guards, and 1st Welsh Guards for overseas service. The aim was for them to move to France immediately, where the Division would form up with those battalions

already deployed. The Guards Division was to have 'no number' and would be quite distinct from others. Kitchener, who had been appointed Colonel of the Irish Guards on the death of Field Marshal Roberts in November 1914, was clearly enthusiastic about the idea of creating a Guards division. In the words of the official historian, 'The loyalty, the discipline, the devotion to duty and the proved efficiency of the Guards would be an example' to all, in particular, perhaps, to the inexperienced officers, non-commissioned officers and soldiers of Kitchener's New Army.

Not everyone shared Kitchener's enthusiasm. There was a view that bringing so many 'fine battalions'

Above top: *King George V.*

Far left: *Lord Kitchener.*

Left: *Lord Cavan.*

Second Lieutenant George Boyd-Rochfort, VC

SCOTS GUARDS

George Boyd-Rochfort was born at Middleton Park House, County Westmeath in 1880. Following his time at Cambridge, he returned to Ireland to run his estate where he was a popular landlord while also spending time big-game hunting, playing polo and competing in horse races. He was seriously injured in a polo accident at the end of August 1914, preventing him from enlisting until the following year, when he joined the Scots Guards, aged 35. He was awarded the VC for his 'conspicuous bravery in the trenches between Cambrin and La Bassée on 3rd August 1915.' His citation was published on 1 September 1915:

> At 2 am a German trench mortar bomb landed on the side of the parapet of the communication trench in which he stood, close to a small working party of his battalion. He might easily have stepped back a few yards round the corner into perfect safety, but, shouting to his men to look out, he rushed at the bomb, seized it and hurled it over the parapet, where it at once exploded. There is no doubt that this splendid combination of presence of mind and courage saved the lives of many of the working party.

George Boyd-Rochfort served on until the end of the war, and was demobilised in 1919. He returned home to the family estate where he became a well-known breeder of race horses. He died in 1940.

together into a single division was a mistake, and that it would be better for their high levels of training and discipline to be more evenly distributed across the BEF. Some Guardsmen felt that the demands of maintaining numbers in an entire division might undermine the Guards' high standards. As one regimental historian commented: 'If the division took a bad knock, the Brigade of Guards might be finished, but as it turned out the division took many bad knocks, but always came up smiling.' Whatever the reservations, the Guards Division formed up in France over the next two months, and was ready to be committed in September.

Field Marshal The 10th Earl of Cavan

GRENADIER GUARDS

Rudolph Lambart was born in 1865, educated at Eton, and commissioned in the Grenadier Guards in 1885. He served at home and overseas, commanding a company during the South African War where he and his men marched 3,000 miles. 'We very rarely saw a Boer,' he later wrote. 'I suppose we heard as many bullets in the whole war as we heard in one day of the 1915–16 battles'. His final posting was to command 1st Battalion Grenadier Guards and he retired from the Army in 1912, becoming Master of the Hertfordshire Hunt. On the outbreak of war in 1914 he re-joined and was soon commanding 4th Guards Brigade during those early days when everyone was struggling to make sense of it all.

The Earl of Cavan (he succeeded to the title in 1900) was a natural leader with an ability to bring order to chaos, and to do it in style. During the First Battle of Ypres there was a moment when just about everything was going wrong: the Germans were about to break through, the GOC 2nd Division was wounded and indisposed, shells were falling on the headquarters, and no one knew what to do for the best. Then Cavan arrived on his horse, dismounted, surveyed the surroundings, slowly drew out his cigar case, selected a cigar, and proceeded to light it while turning it around in his fingers. This act of calmness 'had a wonderful effect on all present, for it not only enabled Lord Cavan himself to concentrate his thoughts on the problem, and to see clearly the most pressing needs of the moment, it also inspired all the officers with confidence'. A staff officer who

was there said afterwards that the cigar saved the situation.

The Earl of Cavan assumed command of the newly formed Guards Division in July 1915, and did so with great pride. 'My men are quite wonderful,' he wrote in a letter home during the Battle of Loos, 'the defence of my line has been a really glorious chapter in the annals of the Guards'. Cavan led the Guards Division until the end of 1915 when he was promoted to command XIV Corps. Fortunately he was not saying goodbye entirely, since the Guards Division was transferred to XIV Corps just a few days later.

In the autumn of 1917 Lord Cavan was summoned by Sir William Robertson, the Chief of the Imperial General Staff (CIGS), to be told: 'Look here Cavan, my lad, you've got to go to Italy and put new heart into our allies. I don't know what the situation may be when you get there but make sure of your line of retreat if things are really bad'. Cavan was soon on his way, along with XIV Corps, to a new front (Italy), a new ally (the Italians), and a new enemy (the Austro-Hungarians). He was shocked by what he found: an Italian army suffering badly from poor leadership and little training in modern warfare. Despite all of this, and in typical style, he was upbeat and confident that the arrival of British troops would have a positive effect on the Italians' morale, and the situation in general.

Cavan remained in Italy for the remainder of the war, and was considering retiring from the Army when a number of appointments came his way. In late 1921 he was asked to be the next CIGS,

CIGS ended, he finally retired and was appointed Colonel of the Irish Guards. On the outbreak of war in 1939, he joined the Hertfordshire Local Defence Volunteers, becoming their Commanding Officer. He died in August 1946.

The Earl of Cavan never attended Staff College, but was well read, travelled widely, and made an effort to learn the languages of the countries where he served. He was, above all, a leader, a gentleman of great charm, someone who believed in order, discipline, and the importance of communicating clearly with his subordinates: a perfect Guardsmen in all respects. To quote a tribute written by General Sir Alexander Godley and published in the *Household Brigade Magazine* in 1946:

> He retained a great simplicity, single-mindedness of purpose, devotion to duty and deep and abiding religious faith which stood him in good stead throughout his whole life; his modesty and sincerity gained him hosts of good friends.

an appointment to which he had not aspired, nor one that he felt particularly qualified to assume. He was looking forward to commanding soldiers again, but felt that, since he had been asked to be CIGS, he should accept. He presided over the Army at a difficult time, during a post-war era of public indifference and defence cuts, and he did much to raise morale throughout the ranks. In February 1924 his term as

Had it not been for the Great War, the Earl of Cavan would have retired to the hunting field having commanded his battalion. As it was, he served throughout the war, later becoming a Field Marshal and CIGS. Then, at the beginning of another war, he was again in command at the age of 70, happily taking up his spade to dig trenches to defend the approaches to Ayot St Lawrence from the invader. A remarkable and fine career.

THE BATTLE OF LOOS

The Battle of Loos is one of those First World War battles that seems to exemplify all the worst aspects of that terrible war. Much was expected of this offensive, 'The Big Push' as it was named at the time, but it was to be a costly and futile endeavour that later provided a touchstone for many of the harshest judgements of the war. The tragedy was that the Allies were still struggling to come to terms with this new kind of warfare. They had yet to grasp the basic mechanics of attacking strong fixed defences; 'attack' seemed the only option.

The year 1915 had been a bad one for the Allies, with France suffering huge casualties and with mounting pressure on the British to do more along the Western Front. Elsewhere, the Gallipoli campaign had foundered and the Germans were gaining on the Eastern Front. At home, Lord Kitchener, Secretary of State for War, had resisted committing his New Army divisions, but now changed his mind. On 19 August, he ordered Sir John French to launch an attack at Loos in support of Joffre's offensive. New Army divisions and the recently formed Guards Division would see action for the first time.

The plan for 'The 'Big Push' was for the British First Army to advance eastwards between the La Bassée Canal and Lens, breaching the German first and second lines of defence and seizing the village of Loos and other strongpoints. As part of a wider offensive, Joffre envisaged a pincer movement that might trap the Germans or force them to withdraw from the Noyon Salient or even push them back beyond the Meuse to end the war. Joffre was confident that the British would 'find particularly favourable ground between Loos and La Bassée'. Sir John French agreed, while Sir Douglas Haig, commanding the First Army, was concerned about the lack of heavy artillery and shells. Sir Henry Rawlinson, a Coldstream Guardsman and one of Haig's corps commanders, noted in his diary, 'My new front is as flat as the palm of my hand. Hardly any cover anywhere . . . It will cost us dearly'. Haig, on visiting the area, recorded his view that 'The ground, for the most part bare and open, would be swept by machine-gun and rifle fire . . . rapid fire would be impossible'.

But Kitchener soon made his views clear: 'we must act with all energy and do our outmost to help France in this offensive, even though by so doing we may suffer very heavy losses'. The British attack on Loos would go ahead regardless; the imperatives were political, not military. Haig decided to attack on a narrow front and with just two divisions, but the prospect of employing gas persuaded him to expand his plan to six divisions over a wider frontage. He requested that the reserves, the Cavalry Corps and XI Corps, with its three infantry divisions (the Guards, 21st, and 24th), be placed under his command before the battle. Sir John French refused, a decision that would later have grave consequences, both for the battle and his future as Commander-in-Chief.

The British artillery barrage began on 21 September, and at 5.50am on 25 September Haig ordered the release of gas from canisters in the front line. The gas clouds lingered in no man's land and in some places drifted back towards the British trenches, causing unnecessary casualties. Forty minutes later, the assaulting infantry began their advance across open fields, and despite heavy losses, by midday had captured the village of Loos and the Hohenzollern Redoubt just to the north. The 21st and 24th Divisions were now called upon to exploit this early success but, due to poor communications and planning, did not go into action until the afternoon of 26 September. Their objective was the strongly held German second-line defences, and in the event the attack was a costly failure with both divisions taking huge casualties.

On 27 September, with the Guards Division now finally under Haig's command, 1st and 2nd Guards Brigades began to relieve the two forward divisions with orders to consolidate the line. Harold Macmillan, who had arrived a few weeks earlier with 4th Grenadiers, recalled the Corps Commander's address prior to the move up to the front line: 'Behind you, gentlemen, in your companies and battalions, will be your Brigadier; behind him your Divisional Commander, and behind you all – I shall be there.' And then came the voice of a fellow officer saying 'Yes, and a long way too!' The Corps Commander was Lieutenant General Richard Haking and in his various addresses he had displayed plenty of enthusiasm for the coming battle, as well as confidence in a favourable outcome. This was going to be 'the greatest battle in the history of the world', and the victors would be the British.

But nothing was going right, and the call for the reserves had been unnecessarily delayed. Conditions for the relief were appalling, the battlefield was strewn with dead bodies and abandoned equipment, and the ground was muddy and slippery. Despite the confusion as the Guards moved forward in darkness, the relief was completed by dawn and they 'had succeeded in making themselves as safe and comfortable as was humanly possible'. Early that afternoon Cavan was ordered to consolidate the British line, with 2nd Guards Brigade capturing Chalk Pit and Puits No. 14.bis on the Lens–La Bassée road, 3rd Guards Brigade capturing Hill 70, and 1st Guards Brigade protecting the left flank.

The ground was flat, and the area beyond the road was particularly exposed to German machine-gun and artillery fire. The three objectives could be clearly seen from where Brigadier General John Ponsonby, commanding 2nd Guards Brigade, issued his orders. It was a particularly bleak and unattractive view, not rolling

Left: *Second Lieutenant Harold Macmillan, Grenadier Guards. Harold Macmillan first became a Member of Parliament in 1924, later served in Winston Churchill's Second World War administration, and was Prime Minister (1957–63).*

Left: *Captain Harold Cuthbert, DSO, Scots Guards. Missing in action at Puits near Loos, 27 September 1915.*

Opposite, right: *Private Peter Larkin, 2nd Battalion, Irish Guards. Killed at Loos, 30 September 1915.*

Opposite, far right: *Second Lieutenant John Kipling, Irish Guards. Wounded and missing at Loos beyond Chalk Pit Wood, 27 September 1915.*

countryside with conveniently placed cover, but a stark coalfield dotted with odd buildings and slag heaps. Puits No. 14.bis was a pithead with a fragile-looking gantry for the winding gear silhouetted on the horizon, described by the Special Correspondent of *The Times* as 'a conspicuous and ugly building with the usual lofty chimney'.

Two companies of 2nd Irish Guards moved off at 4pm, and reached Chalk Pit Wood with only a few casualties, having been protected by a smokescreen laid by 1st Guards Brigade. They then joined 2nd Scots Guards as they 'advanced in open order and doubled downhill under very heavy fire of shrapnel'. Reinforced unexpectedly by a detachment of 4th Grenadiers, the Scots and Irish then assaulted the 'Keep' objective and the Puits. A small party of Scots Guards managed to get inside the building where there was some 'fierce hand-to-hand fighting with the Germans' but casualties had been so heavy that success

was not possible. Meanwhile, 1st Coldstream following up 2nd Irish Guards and 3rd Grenadier Guards supporting 2nd Scots Guards had come under fire as they advanced towards Chalk Pit Wood. A few Grenadiers managed to reach the Puits, but along with the Scots Guards were forced to pull back. By the end of the day 2nd Guards Brigade had achieved some success by securing Chalk Pit Wood, but at considerable cost, and the toll in officers was particularly high. Puits had been beyond their grasp. To quote the Scots Guards regimental history: 'It was a great achievement, in the face of the terrible fire, to have gained the position at all; it would have been a greater one to hold it; for the position had been so completely prepared and covered by fire by the Germans that it was almost untenable by any British who got into it.'

Rudyard Kipling, in his history of the 2nd Battalion Irish Guards, quotes the war diary, describing how 'some few Irish Guardsmen', including his son John Kipling, had gone forward with the Scots Guards party commanded by Captain Harold Cuthbert. This 'rush' of Guardsmen somehow made it to a line beyond the Puits, but in the face of heavy machine-gun fire. Captain Cuthbert was dead, young Kipling was wounded and missing, and the Scots Guards party fell back from the Puits 'into and through Chalk-Pit Wood in some confusion'. But there were still some Irish Guardsmen beyond the wood; a little later, a runner was despatched by Captain Harold Alexander, 'saying that he and some men were still in their scratch-trenches on the far side of Chalk-Pit Wood,

and he would be greatly obliged if they would kindly send some more men up, with speed', although, as Kipling observes, the 'actual language was somewhat crisper'.

The 3rd Guards Brigade attack on to Hill 70 was to take place once Chalk Pit Wood and Puits had been captured, since the risk of enfilade fire from these positions was too great. But Brigadier General Heyworth went ahead with the attack unaware that Puits remained in enemy hands. The brigade began their advance having been warned that as soon as they 'appeared over the skyline beyond Fosse No. 7 they would probably come under the enemy's artillery fire'. The warning was to prove correct, but despite 'a tornado of shrapnel fire', in the words of *The Times*' Special Correspondent, the brigade:

> advanced with the steadiness of men on parade, and men of other battalions who could see the manoeuvre from their own trenches have spoken again and again of that wonderful advance as being one of the most glorious and impressive sights of the war, and how they were thrilled to see those large silhouettes pressing silently and inexorably forward against the skyline.

As the brigade marched forward, to quote the Welsh Guards' regimental history,

> shrapnel burst, making puffs of smoke overhead, high explosive shells sent up sudden fountains of mud and black smoke which completely obliterated, according to the view-point, now one, now another of those small squares of advancing men, who, however, slowly and steadily continued to advance, the brigade covering a large area of ground in this formation.

A soldier watching from the nearby Royal Sussex Regiment's trenches described their advance as bringing 'tears to my eyes, men were dropping like flies but they kept on as if they were marching up the Mall'.

The brigade managed to reach the houses in Loos in remarkably good order, although 4th Grenadiers were met with a volley of gas shells as they emerged from the communication trenches close to the village. In the confusion, as soldiers donned their Hypo helmets, the Commanding Officer became a gas casualty and over half the battalion was separated from the remainder in the narrow streets. Harold Macmillan and his platoon were among them and, reluctant to crawl, he described 'walking about, trying to look as self-possessed as possible, under heavy fire'. Another Grenadier officer saw the artillery commander in Loos 'almost demented' because of the lack of infantry in the village and then 'regardless by shot and shell, Harold, aged 21, walking up and down the roads in full view of the enemy, holding the General by the arm and saying his men would be there in a few minutes and all would be well'. Macmillan had already been slightly wounded in the head, and was later shot in the right hand and evacuated. For a while after the battle, all acts of courage were rated by the 4th Grenadiers as 'nearly as brave as Mr Macmillan'.

With 4th Grenadiers now much reduced in numbers, Brigadier General Heyworth decided to give the task of capturing Hill 70 to 1st Welsh Guards, supported by the Grenadiers. Making the assumption that the Puits had been captured by the Scots Guards, he briefed the Welsh Guards' Commanding Officer, Lieutenant Colonel Murray-Threipland. The Welsh Guards had also experienced their first gas attack that afternoon as they struggled into their new 'horrible slimy bags', the Hypo helmets. Captain Humphrey Dene later recalled the scene, as the battalion made 'noises like frogs

and penny tin trumpets as they spat and blew down the tubes of their helmets [as] shells crashed into houses'.

Murray-Threipland went off to find the Grenadiers, made his plan and gave orders to his company commanders. The attack on Hill 70 began at 5.30pm and was under way when Murray-Threipland was informed that it was to be cancelled due to the failure to capture Puits. It was, of course, too late, and in the event good progress was made until the Guards reached the crest of Hill 70, when they came under intensive machine-gun fire. Private Britton described the experience: 'I was a bit flurried but soon got over it. We had to advance along a communication trench where there were most elaborately fitted dug-outs. I saw a dead German with his head and leg blown off'.

Despite the intensive machine-gun fire, the Welsh Guards and Grenadiers managed to get within 25 yards

of the enemy position. Heyworth had given orders that no one was to go beyond the crest, but sadly the order had not reached Major Myles Ponsonby, now commanding the Grenadiers. Consequently, they took very heavy casualties on Hill 70, including Ponsonby himself who was hit and died the following morning. His adjutant, Captain Thomas Thorne, who had dressed Ponsonby's wounds as he lay just 25 yards from the German position, was killed later that day, trying to carry a wounded drummer to safety.

Sometime later, Murray-Threipland sent the message that Hill 70 had been successfully taken, requesting that 2nd Scots Guards should relieve the Welsh Guards and Grenadiers in order to consolidate the position. Lieutenant Colonel Albemarle Cator, commanding the Scots Guards, decided to establish a line 100 yards further back since no proper digging could be

conducted so close to the German position on the crest. The trenches were quickly dug and well wired, but the gathering-in of the wounded lying below the crest was all but impossible. The area was now more secure than before the attack, and the Welsh Guards, ably supported by the Grenadiers and Scots Guards, had seen action for the first time. But the losses in 3rd Guards Brigade, particularly among officers, had been high, and the redoubt on top of the hill was still held by the Germans.

Lord Cavan decided that further attacks on Hill 70 would serve no purpose, and so gave orders that the defences around the hill were to be strengthened. In the meantime, he received orders that the Guards Division was to conduct an attack on to Puits No. 14.bis on the afternoon of 28 September. Brigadier General Ponsonby, commanding 2nd Guards Brigade, believed that the attack had little chance of success, but since he had no communications with Lord Cavan, felt obliged to carry on. The attack was conducted by the Coldstream Guards in the face of heavy machine-gun fire from three directions. A few soldiers reached the Puits, but the attack proved to be abortive, with 9 officers and 250 other ranks killed or wounded.

The Guards Division now consolidated their positions, extending their trenches to secure the new front line. Working throughout the hours of darkness on the night of 30 September, 1st and 2nd Guards Brigades dug trenches along the Lens–La Bassée road, linking up close to the Chalk Pit. Concurrently, the relief of the Guards Division began at midnight on 30 September, and was completed by 4am the following day, despite heavy shelling, appalling weather, and dreadful conditions on the ground. Three days later, the Guards Division was called forward again, this time to be prepared to conduct an attack on to the Quarries, over 2 miles to the north of its old positions. By 4.15am on 6 October, this complicated 'side-slip' of the brigades had been completed. Orders had also been received for gas cylinders to be brought forward to the front line in preparation for the attack.

Sometime around 4pm on 8 October, the Germans launched an attack along 2nd Guards Brigade's front line, with most of the attack concentrating just south of the Hohenzollern Redoubt. Two companies of 3rd Grenadiers were attacked along a communication trench running east and west of their positions, and soon they had exhausted their supply of hand grenades (known as 'bombs'.) The turning point of the engagement came with the action of Lance Sergeant Oliver Brooks of 3rd Coldstream who organised a 'bombing party' and proceeded to drive the Germans back, bombing them out of their trenches. By 7pm the line had been recovered and positions consolidated. For this brave action, Lance Sergeant Brooks was later awarded the VC.

The official history identifies two factors in the reversal of fortunes that afternoon: firstly, the action of the bombers so ably led by Lance Sergeant Oliver Brooks, and secondly, the supply of grenades from 1st Irish Guards on their left which had allowed the fighting to continue. The relative ease with which brigades and battalions helped and supported each other demonstrated one of the advantages that the Guards Division had over other formations. Even though this was a new division, there was already a sense of unity and common training and a 'feeling of confidence and pride which is bound up in the traditions of the Brigade of Guards'.

On 12 October, just before a planned relief, the Guards Division was again attacked by the Germans.

Following a tough four-hour battle, which combined bombing and the firing of trench mortars, the Germans pulled back having gained no ground and incurring heavy casualties. By 14 October, the Guards were again back in the front line, preparing for another attack, this time on to the Dump and Fosse trenches. Conditions were appalling. To quote the war diary of 1st Coldstream:

> The state of the trenches was terrible, unburied bodies lying everywhere, and the parapets and communication trenches blown in on all sides. The trenches allotted to the battalion were knocked about and we found dead bodies, equipment and debris of all kinds mixed up together. Salvage parties worked all day. Just as much damage was done to the communication trenches as the front line trench.

Digging was extremely difficult and dangerous. 'Work could only be done at night', wrote Evelyn Fryer, serving with 3rd Grenadiers, 'and then one could only sap and not dig from the top, and the Germans were only a few yards off, and it meant certain death to show oneself.'

The Battle of Loos was not yet over. By 17 October, 2nd and 3rd Guards Brigades were back in the front line, preparing for an attack on to the Hohenzollern Redoubt. It began at 5am, supported by artillery and trench mortars. But in the face of intensive enfilade machine-gun fire, Lord Cavan called off the attack at 8am. The decision had clearly not been taken lightly. To quote the official history:

> Some idea of the severity of the fighting may be obtained from the fact that the two Guards brigades between them made use of 15,000 bombs, while both brigadiers agreed that they had experienced no more heavy shell fire during the war than between dawn and midday on the 17th [October 1915].

Lieutenant General Sir Francis Lloyd, Grenadier Guards

'THE MAN WHO RUNS LONDON'

Major General Sir Francis Lloyd became General Officer Commanding London District and the Brigade of Guards in September 1913 at the age of 60 at the end of a long and successful career. In peacetime he might have expected a few busy but predictable years in the post, but from August 1914, Lloyd's responsibilities broadened considerably. He oversaw the hospitals, the security of London, and the training and readiness of the Guards regiments at home, among many other tasks, including, later in the war, the construction of trenches to encircle the capital.

Lloyd, a Welshman, took a keen interest in the formation of the Welsh Guards in 1915, telling one newspaper: 'What we have to do is to get Welsh soldiers for the Guards, because you cannot begin such a regiment with a lot of recruits. It is going to be a Guards regiment for the King, not merely a regiment of Welshmen, and we must have the right type of man, and such a regiment of Welshmen will fight, like the very devil'. He called upon Welshmen in his own regiment to step forward and transfer, and within a few days he told the newspapers that the nucleus of the Welsh Guards had been formed. 'They are all typical Welshmen, and many of them speak the language. They are all Evanses and Joneses and Davieses and Lloyds. We are out, in fact, to make this a characteristically Welsh regiment'.

London was a prime target for German air raids with the first Zeppelins dropping high explosive and incendiary bombs on the East End in May 1915, with more raids to follow and mounting casualties.

Gradually the Zeppelins lost their edge as defences improved, but then came the Gotha bombers, flying higher and faster. In June 1917 Lloyd attended the funerals of 16 children killed in a raid on Poplar, and was much moved by the sight of the coffins lined up in the church. Later that summer, he told Londoners not to do 'what I'm afraid I did – go and look and see what is going on' when there was an air raid. His advice was 'to go down into the Tubes' for safety.

Francis Lloyd became the most well-known military figure in London during the war, often out and about doing his part to bring comfort and support to Londoners. He finally retired on 1 October 1918 in the rank of Lieutenant General, later becoming a London County Council member and the Food Commissioner for London and the Home Counties. He died in February 1926 at his home in Chigwell, Essex.

There were other tactical lessons from Loos, but not all were identified at the time. The battle fits many of the stereotypes by which later generations have judged the competence of the senior commanders, most notably French and Haig. Tactics were still evolving, but progress was slow as commanders at all levels struggled with the demands of modern warfare. Rudyard Kipling expresses understandable emotion in describing the fighting in which his own son John was killed:

The Loos offensive ended the following day. The British had begun with a numerical advantage, but the ground was far more favourable to the Germans, there were shortages of heavy artillery and shells, and the use of gas created as many problems for the attacker as the defender. The reserves had been held back from the front line and remained under Sir John French's orders for too long, a fact that Haig wasted no time in reporting to Kitchener: 'No Reserve was placed under me. My attack, as has been reported, was a complete success. The enemy had no troops in his second line, which some of my plucky fellows reached and entered without opposition.' But by the time the reserves were ready to attack, it was too late. 'We were in a position to make this the turning point in the war . . . but naturally I feel very annoyed at the lost opportunity.'

So, when the Press was explaining to a puzzled public what a far reaching success had been achieved, the 'greatest battle in the history of the world' simmered down to picking up the pieces on both sides of the line, and a return to autumnal trench-work, until more and heavier guns could be designed and manufactured in England. Meanwhile, men died.

Above: *Ruins of Loos after the battle.*

Right: *Lieutenant John Kipling's grave in St Mary's Cemetery in Haisnes, France. Kipling disappeared during the Battle of Loos and was still listed as missing at the end of the war. The body of an unidentified Irish Guards lieutenant was found in 1919 but it was not until 1992 that the Commonwealth War Graves Commission were sufficiently confident that it was 'Jack' Kipling to erect a headstone for him. Rudyard never forgave himself for having facilitated his son's entry into the Army, despite poor eyesight having been the cause of his earlier rejection.*

The Guards Division had fought bravely at Loos, earning many fine tributes from observers, including the Special Correspondent of *The Times*. The words used to describe the Guards in action resonated with the image of the parade ground and public duties, faded picture postcards of tunics, bearskins, and soldiers marching steadily in perfect formation. The public back home would not have been disappointed; the Guards had fought well. But casualties had been heavy, particularly in 1st Scots Guards, who had lost 474 soldiers. Many officers and non-commissioned officers, pre-war regulars and reservists who had been fighting since August 1914, were dead, and there was a gradual acknowledgement that the reserve officers replacing them were now earning their spurs at the front. To quote the official history, 'After the Battle of Loos, even old-fashioned Guardsmen became convinced that officers of the Special Reserve could safely be employed as company commanders.' The reality was that from now on, and increasingly, it would be the reservists who would be in the lead, since so many of the old regulars were gone.

British losses at Loos were nearly 50,000, with 16,000 dead and 25,000 wounded. It was to be Sir John French's last major battle. The knives were already out, and he was now left with few friends in high places. Criticism steadily grew in the weeks that followed, and the Commander-in-Chief's official despatch, published on 2 November 1915, did little to relieve the mounting pressure. By early December, French was appealing to Herbert Asquith, but the Prime Minister, now heavily influenced by the views of many others, made it known that French must resign, which he did. On 10 December 1915, Haig was informed that he was to be appointed Commander-in-Chief.

Six months later, on 6 June 1916, Sir John French was appointed Colonel of the Irish Guards, succeeding Lord Kitchener who had been drowned the previous day when the armoured cruiser HMS *Hampshire* hit a mine and sank west of the Orkney Islands. Although some Irish Guardsmen became a little ambivalent about Sir John French's legacy, he is now remembered for one important reason: he saved the regiment from disbandment in the early 1920s. To quote the *Household Brigade Magazine* in 1925, following his death, 'the younger generation of Irish Guardsmen should realise that had it not been for their Colonel's determined stand through the controversy of 1920 their Regiment would by now have in all probability ceased to exist as a Regiment'.

Right: *Company Sergeant Major Toher receiving a Military Medal from Field Marshal Viscount French (later The Earl of Ypres), Colonel, Irish Guards, St Patrick's Day, 1917. CSM Toher's description of a British artillery barrage at the front was to become famous in the Regiment: 'And even the wurrums themselves are getting up and crying for mercy'.*

Winston Churchill visits the Grenadier Guards
NOVEMBER–DECEMBER 1915

Winston Churchill, out of political office for the first time in 13 years, crossed to France on 18 November 1915 to join the Oxfordshire Hussars. At Boulogne he was intercepted by Sir John French's staff, and at General Headquarters that evening French suggested he should become one of his aide-de-camps or be given a brigade. Churchill seized upon the latter, asking that first he receive some training with the Guards. Two days later, Lord Cavan informed him that he would be attached to 2nd Battalion Grenadier Guards, commanded by Lieutenant Colonel 'Ma' Jeffreys.

Churchill's escorting officer was Major 'Bulgy' Thorne, who recalled that on arrival at Battalion HQ he 'had never seen a more hostile looking lot and I was sorry to leave him to his fate'. Churchill remembered 'the Colonel' saying 'I think I ought to tell you that we were not at all consulted in the matter of your coming to join us', followed, after a long silence, by the Adjutant informing him that 'I am afraid that we have had to cut down your kit rather, Major. There are no communication trenches here. We are doing all our reliefs over the top. The men have little more than what they stand up in.'

That first evening, the Grenadiers moved into the front line just north of Neuve Chapelle. Following dinner Churchill set off to find a place to sleep. He rejected the small signal office, 'occupied by four busy Morse signallers', and following an inspection of the only alternative on offer, 'a sort of pit four feet deep, containing about a foot of water', Churchill was back with the signallers for the night.

Writing to his wife Clementine, Churchill described his first day in the front line, a place of 'great tranquillity' apart from the occasional stray bullet and some sniping. Despite his inauspicious welcome, his first impressions were favourable: 'I am not going to be in a hurry to leave the regiment while it is in the line, as its Colonel is one of the very best in the army and his knowledge of trench warfare is complete and profound. All his comments and instruction to his men are pregnant with military wisdom; and the system of the Guards – discipline and hard work – must be seen at close quarters to be fully admired as it deserves'.

The front line was grim, with frequent shelling, appalling weather, and ragged trenches. 'The Guards are cleaning everything up,' wrote Churchill, 'and work day and night to strengthen the parapet and improve the shelter. The neglect and idleness of the former tenants is obvious at every step. Filth and rubbish everywhere, graves built into the defences and scattered about promiscuously, feet and clothing breaking through the soil, water and muck on all sides and about the scene in the dazzling moonlight troops of enormous rats creep and glide to the unceasing accompaniment of rifles and machine guns and the venomous whining and whirring of bullets which pass over head'.

Churchill was happy: 'Amid these surroundings, aided by wet and cold, and every minor discomfort, I have found happiness and content such as I have not known for many months'. Back in reserve billets, he wrote to his wife: 'I am making friends with the officers and the Colonel, and it is pleasant to see their original doubts and prejudices fading away. The discipline and organisation of their battalions is admirable. In spite of losses which have left hardly a dozen of the original personnel remaining, and repeated refills from various sources, the tradition and the system of the Guards asserts itself in hard work, smartness and soldierly behaviour. It will always be a memorable experience to me to have served with them'.

On 15 December, just before Churchill left the Grenadiers, he recounted an extraordinary incident to his wife: 'Ten Grenadiers under a kid went across by night to the German Trench which they found largely deserted or waterlogged. They fell upon a picket of Germans, beat the brains out of two of them and dragged a third triumphantly home as a prisoner. The young officer by accident let off his pistol and shot one of his own Grenadiers dead: but the others kept this secret and pretended it was done by the enemy – do likewise. Such men you never saw. The scene in the little dugout when the prisoner was brought in surrounded by these terrific warriors, in jerkins and steel helmets with their bloody clubs in hand – looking pictures of ruthless war – was one to stay in the memory. *C'est tres bon.* They petted the prisoner and gave him cigarettes and tried to cheer him up. He was not very unhappy to be taken and knew he would be safe and well fed until the end of the war'. The young 'kid' was Lieutenant the Honourable William Parnell, who was awarded an MC. He was killed, aged 22, in September 1916.

On collecting Churchill at the end of the attachment, 'Bulgy' Thorne found an entirely different atmosphere:

Left: *Winston Churchill in France. While serving with 2nd Battalion Grenadier Guards in September 1915, he wrote in a letter to his wife: 'My (French) steel helmet is the cause of much envy. I look most martial in it – like a Cromwellian – I always intend to wear it under fire – but chiefly for the appearance'.*

'there was W.S.C. holding forth with pink and blue Tories alike hanging on his lips. His character and military prescience had won them over and he had surely demonstrated his fitness for command in the field'.

Churchill never got his brigade; despite Sir John French's attempts, there was little support from elsewhere. On New Year's Day 1916, Churchill was informed that he would command 6th Battalion Royal Scots Fusiliers. But he never forgot the Grenadiers, the friends he made and his experiences with them in the front line in late 1915.

Lance Sergeant Oliver Brooks, vc

COLDSTREAM GUARDS

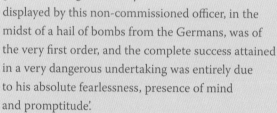

Oliver Brooks was born in Paulton, Somerset, in 1889, and as a boy worked in the Somerset coal pits, drawing coal trucks by a chain harnessed around his waist. He enlisted in the Coldstream Guards in 1906, and having completed his seven years' service, he transferred to the reserve in 1913, becoming a manager of a cinema/theatre at Peasedown. In August 1914 he was back with the Coldstream Guards, on his way to France with 3rd Battalion. He was promoted to Lance Corporal three months later, and in July 1915 became a Lance Sergeant.

On 8 October 1915 Lance Sergeant Oliver Brooks showed conspicuous bravery during the Battle of Loos and was awarded the VC for his actions. His citation was published on 28 October 1915: 'A strong party of the enemy having captured 200 yards of our trenches, Lance Sergeant Oliver Brooks, on his own initiative, led a party of bombers in the most determined manner, and succeeded in regaining possession of the lost ground. The signal bravery displayed by this non-commissioned officer, in the midst of a hail of bombs from the Germans, was of the very first order, and the complete success attained in a very dangerous undertaking was entirely due to his absolute fearlessness, presence of mind and promptitude'.

Oliver Brooks was promoted to sergeant on the day following this brave action. He received his VC on 1 November 1915 from King George V while on a visit to France. The King had been thrown from his horse and was on a hospital train at the time and confined to his bed. Brooks knelt on the floor next to the bed, while the King struggled to pin the medal through Brooks' thick tunic.

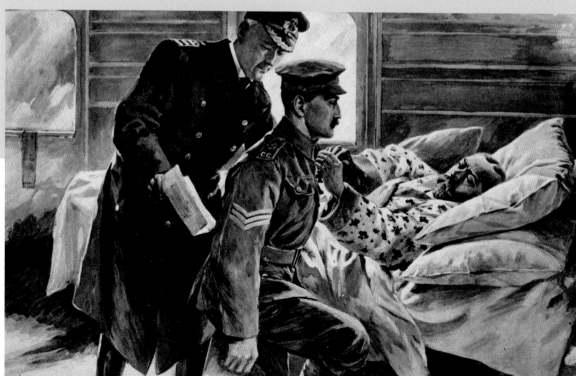

The BEF began to take over the French front line running through the Somme area in mid-1915, and at the end of the year there were discussions about a joint Anglo–French offensive there in the summer of 1916. Initial plans involved a major role for the French, fielding twice as many divisions as the British who were arguably still not ready to commit their New Army divisions to a major offensive. Around December 1915, at the end of a dismal year of attrition and no real progress, the Allies grasped at the hope that a massive attack on either side of the River Somme would deliver the breakthrough that had so far eluded them.

Sergeant Brooks was wounded in the head and shoulder at Ginchy in September 1916, making a good recovery. Later in the war, as a bombing instructor, one of his pupils was the Prince of Wales, who, he said, 'became very proficient' at the art of trench bombing, the same skill for which Brooks had been awarded his VC.

After the war, Oliver Brooks became a commissionaire at the White Hart Hotel in Windsor and later at the Dorchester Hotel in London, where, in April 1933, the ex-Kaiser's grandson shook him by the hand with the words 'Every nation can recognise a brave man'. He died on 25 October 1940 in Windsor, where he is buried.

Opposite: *Sergeant Brooks being presented with his VC by King George V from a hospital bed on a train.*

Right: *General Sir Henry Rawlinson, a Coldstream Guardsman, who commanded the British Fourth Army during the Battle of the Somme.*

1916

On 21 February 1916, the Germans launched a major attack on Verdun. The French were now no longer able to defend themselves there while also taking on a major offensive elsewhere. What had started as a joint venture on the Somme had become a British-led attack with, hopefully, some peripheral support from the French. Furthermore, Haig was now placed under considerable pressure by the French to bring forward the date of the Somme offensive from mid-August to late June. While there had been much preparation for this battle over the previous six months, on a scale hitherto unprecedented, the Germans held many of the cards, despite the pressures they were experiencing around Verdun. Since late 1914, when they had seized ground most suitable for the defence, the Germans had been steadily strengthening their positions and strongpoints along the Somme front. They were also fully aware of the feverish activity on the other side of the line. The British attack, whenever it came, would not be a surprise to the Germans; they were expecting it.

The Battle of the Somme began on 1 July 1916, having been preceded by a week-long artillery barrage that would have dispelled any German doubts about the impending attack. Huge mines had been laid by the Royal Engineers beneath the German front line, and frequent trench and aerial raids had been conducted in the weeks leading up to zero hour. There was great confidence among the infantry units of the Fourth (British) Army, many of whom had never seen action before. But the opening battles were to be bitterly disappointing, with only local and limited successes along the front. While the British artillery inflicted considerable damage on the German positions at ground level, undermining morale and logistical supply to the front line, the second and third-line defences remained largely intact as did the deep underground strongholds that had been constructed in the solid chalk below.

Welsh Guards in a reserve trench at Guillemont on the Somme, September 1916.

THE BATTLE OF THE SOMME

When, at zero hour, 7.30am on 1 July 1916, the British artillery fell silent, the Germans emerged from their deep dugouts to man their damaged trenches and well-sited machine-gun posts. The effect on the advancing British infantry was devastating and while there was some success in the south, the overall picture at the end of the first day was little short of disastrous, with 57,470 British casualties which included 19,240 dead. Despite these terrible losses, Haig had no alternative but to continue with the offensive. By 11 July the front-line German trenches had been taken, but progress was slow and costly, and where there were local successes, it was rarely possible for them to be exploited.

During most of July 1916, the Guards Division remained in the Ypres Salient and while 'no sane man was personally anxious to take part in the [Somme] offensive, there was yet a feeling throughout the division that the proper place for the Guards was in the battle zone'. Nearly nine months had passed since the Battle of Loos, a period when the Guards had been involved only

in small-scale raids and trench routine, and the new GOC, Major General Geoffrey Feilding was keen for the division to get back into action.

On 27 July, the Guards Division was relieved by 4th Division in the Boesinghe sector of Flanders and began to make its way south towards the Somme. Three days later the Divisional HQ was established at Doullens, with the brigades billeted close by. On 9 August, the same day that the King, accompanied by the Prince of Wales, visited the division, the relief into a reserve area, some 4 miles to the east, took place. Two weeks later, the Guards Division moved further south by road and rail, transferring to Rawlinson's Fourth Army. On 25 August, the division rejoined Lord Cavan's XIV Corps, with the divisional headquarters at Treux, 4 miles south-west of Albert. Here they remained for a further ten days, as corps reserve. It was an opportunity for battalion training, interspersed with brigade exercises coordinated at divisional level to ensure a common tactical approach by all units. Special emphasis was placed on signalling: the use of pigeons, additional runners for each battalion, and a 'single trunk system to the most advanced point possible', a concept that seemed more sensible and easier to maintain than multiple telephone lines trailing across the battlefield.

On 3 September 1916, a conference was held at Divisional HQ at which Major General Feilding explained the overall plan. The Fourth Army's renewed advance would begin on 15 September, with the Guards, together with the 6th and 56th Divisions, attacking enemy positions between Ginchy and Flers. Two Guards

Left: *Field Marshal Sir Douglas Haig, Commander-in-Chief BEF from December 1915; Colonel of the Royal Horse Guards, 1919–28.*

Above: *Transport horses and wagons in difficulties in a muddy area on the Somme, July 1916.*

Right: *Staff officers being presented to King George V at Guards Division Headquarters, Chocques, August 1916.*

brigades would advance on a narrow 1,000-yard frontage, and Feilding decided to concentrate his infantry in the front ranks, in the hope that they would miss the worst of the German artillery barrage in depth. The reserve brigade would follow on as quickly as possible.

As a preliminary to the main attack, 3rd Guards Brigade moved into the front line, at night. 4th Grenadiers completed their move to the south-east of the badly damaged Ginchy on 10 September, and under constant artillery fire found their new trenches to be 'broken and disconnected . . . and filled with the dead of the 47th Infantry Brigade'. The Welsh Guards, on the outskirts of Ginchy and out of touch with the Grenadiers to the south, found themselves being counter-attacked just as they had taken over their trenches. With reinforcements from a company of 4th Grenadiers, the Welsh Guards managed to reorganise and regain some of their lost ground, and were then relieved the following night. At 2am on 12 September,

2nd Company, 4th Grenadiers, commanded by Captain A. C. Graham, was ordered to 'bomb its way across the gap in the line south-east of Ginchy'. The company, composed of a combination of bombing and blocking parties, carrying an array of grenades, sandbags, shovels and spare small-arms ammunition, managed to advance to within 100 yards of its objective in the face of intensive machine-gun fire. Captain Graham was killed later during the advance and, unable to get further, the company blocked the trench with sandbags in an attempt to secure the line.

The Albert Medal

The Albert Medal, named after the Prince Consort, was introduced in 1866 for gallantry in saving life at sea. In 1877 the scope was broadened, and in effect it became the highest award for bravery 'not in the face of the enemy'. During the Great War 154 Albert Medals were awarded, of which many involved mishaps with explosives. In the Guards, one was awarded posthumously to a second lieutenant in the Scots Guards, two to lance corporals in the Grenadier Guards, and one to a private in the Coldstream Guards.

Lance Corporal Percy Warwick
Grenadier Guards

On 19 September 1915, while serving in France, Lance Corporal Percy Warwick was instructing a class in throwing live grenades from a saphead into a small trench 25 yards away. One of the men under instruction was nervous, and, after igniting his grenade, dropped it behind him. Warwick immediately picked it up and threw it out of the trench, where it exploded. He was presented with the Albert Medal by King George V at Buckingham Palace on 21 March 1916. Warwick was discharged from the Army on demobilisation in March 1920. He died in 1959 at the age of 74.

2nd Lieutenant Grey De Lèche Leach
Scots Guards

At Morlancourt, on 3 September 1916, Grey de Lèche Leach, the Bombing Officer of 1st Battalion Scots Guards, was inserting detonators in bombs in the Orderly Room when the fuse of one of the bombs accidentally ignited. There were others in the room and outside, so, unable to throw the bomb away, he pressed it close to his body until it exploded. He died of his wounds aged 22 and, in recognition of his gallantry, he was posthumously awarded the Albert Medal in Gold, of which only 70 were awarded. It was presented to his father by the King at Buckingham Palace on 9 February 1918.

Lance Corporal William Meredith
Grenadier Guards

On 5 November 1916, Lance Corporal William Meredith was instructing a class in firing live rifle grenades. When a soldier fired a grenade from his rifle, the charge was insufficient to project the grenade, and the soldier held onto the rifle instead of throwing it down. Meredith threw himself in front of the soldier and attempted to remove the grenade, but it exploded. He lost three fingers of his right hand and was wounded in nine other places. He was medically discharged from the Army the following year, receiving the Silver War Badge, given to all those who were discharged because of

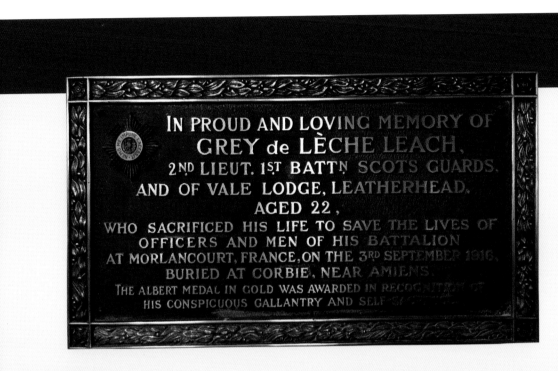

IN PROUD AND LOVING MEMORY OF
GREY de LÈCHE LEACH,
2ND LIEUT. 1ST BATTN SCOTS GUARDS,
AND OF VALE LODGE, LEATHERHEAD.
AGED 22,
WHO SACRIFICED HIS LIFE TO SAVE THE LIVES OF
OFFICERS AND MEN OF HIS BATTALION
AT MORLANCOURT, FRANCE, ON THE 3RD SEPTEMBER 1916,
BURIED AT CORBIE, NEAR AMIENS.
THE ALBERT MEDAL IN GOLD WAS AWARDED IN RECOGNITION OF
HIS CONSPICUOUS GALLANTRY AND SELF-SACRIFICE

Above: *The memorial to Grey De Lèche Leach in the Parish Church of St Mary and St Nicholas, Leatherhead.*

Opposite: *The Albert Medal.*

wounds or illness. In July 1918 Meredith wrote to Regimental Headquarters to enquire if details of these acts of bravery had been documented. This provoked some correspondence which led to a corroboration of the full facts, leading to the recommendation of the Albert Medal. On 7 February 1919, Meredith's award was approved by King George V, and two weeks later he received it at Buckingham Palace.

Private James Dunn Coldstream Guards

Private James Dunn was at a railhead on 12 June 1918 when several trucks loaded with heavy ammunition caught fire. Dunn rushed forward, carrying two wounded men to a shelter trench where he gave them first aid. He continued to help the other wounded, even when there was a second explosion. James Dunn was awarded the Albert Medal on 30 August 1918, and was later employed as the orderly to the Major General Commanding the Brigade of Guards.

In 1971, the Albert Medal was discontinued and the surviving holders were invited to exchange them for the George Cross. Many accepted the offer, but William Meredith did not, on the grounds that since he had received his Albert Medal from the King, this was the one he would keep.

The Guards Entrenching Battalion

Entrenching battalions were formed in the autumn of 1915 to dig trenches and carry out other manual work behind the lines. In the early days Guardsmen were posted indiscriminately to these battalions, but in December 1915, a special Guards Entrenching Battalion, under the command of Major E. C. Ellice, Grenadier Guards, was formed. For the next six months leading up the Somme offensive, the battalion was based not far from Albert, digging trenches, dugouts and artillery positions. During the fighting that began in July 1916, it moved forward to the area of Mametz to build gun emplacements for the French artillery, and by December 1916 it was based in Trônes Wood. The following spring the battalion was building new trenches and strongpoints and working on the water supply and telephone lines around Combles, Ginchy and Lesbœufs, all areas well-known to the Guards Division from the fighting the previous year. Prior to the Cambrai offensive, the battalion was again at the front digging trenches and laying narrow-gauge Decauville railway lines.

The entrenching battalions were disbanded in the late summer of 1917, but in October Major General Feilding raised a Reinforcements Battalion to serve a similar purpose. When questions from above were asked about its role, the name was changed to the Guards Works Battalion which seem to satisfy the chain of command for a while. It continued to play a useful role in early 1918, and the system of exchanges set up with the front-line battalions allowed men to get a well-earned rest away from the action.

In April 1918, there came more objections from senior officers, and the battalion was finally reduced to a small cadre. During its short existence, 344 officers and about 10,000 soldiers had passed through the Guards Entrenching Battalion. It had proved to be an invaluable unit, not only for the tasks it undertook, but as a source of readily available individual reinforcements close to the front line.

Left: *Grenadier Guards building a road near Albert, September 1916.*

GINCHY

During the night of 12–13 September, 3rd Guards Brigade was relieved by 1st and 2nd Guards Brigades, and final preparations took place for the main attack two days later. The Guards Division, as part of Lord Cavan's XIV Corps, would be attacking on the left, from a line running just north-east of Ginchy towards Lesbœufs. In his briefing, Feilding emphasised the importance of quickly overcoming any resistance close to Ginchy, since this would be vital to the overall success of the later battle. This initial phase was a considerable concern to the Divisional Commander, perhaps because so many of the Somme offensives had foundered early in the attack. 'This is perhaps the greatest battle that has ever been fought', said Feilding. 'The Guards Division has been specially selected for the operation, the eyes of the whole of England will be watching us and I have absolute confidence that we shall live up to our reputation.'

In the very early hours of 15 September, a cold night, 1st and 2nd Guards Brigades were in their assembly areas ready to move off, with 3rd Brigade in reserve behind. It would be a difficult advance, as the Guards Division's starting point around the eastern side of Ginchy was semicircular and could easily have become dangerously exposed and reliant upon the two flanking divisions. At 6.20am the infantry attack began behind a creeping barrage of British artillery fire, an innovation that had been introduced since the opening Somme battles.

There were problems from the outset, as the German infantry and machine-gunners fought from collapsed trenches and shell-holes, and the 6th Division's advance to the north of Ginchy faltered. With enfilade fire coming from the south-eastern corner of the village, 3rd Grenadiers set up a defensive flank on the right of the advance, while 1st Coldstream found themselves underneath the British creeping barrage, losing its

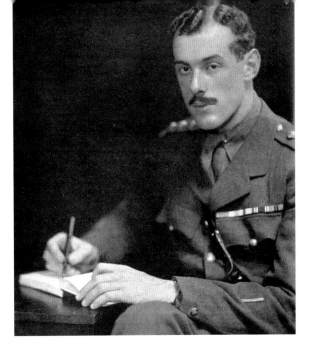

Above: *Captain Oliver Lyttelton, Adjutant, 3rd Grenadiers. Oliver Lyttelton became a Member of Parliament in 1940, served in Winston Churchill's Second World War administration and, as Lord Chandos, became the first chairman of the National Theatre (1962–72).*

bearings. A combination of these factors, together with intensive German machine-gun fire, caused great confusion for 2nd Guards Brigade, with officers and men fighting in small groups. Oliver Lyttelton, the Adjutant, 3rd Grenadiers, 'saw Scots Guards, Coldstreamers, Irish Guards and our own fellows all mixed up. But no one cared. We were getting a fair number of shells among us and not a few bullets. The dust and the smoke hid everything.' Somehow, 3rd Grenadiers and 1st Coldstream, with support from other battalions, managed to reach their first objective.

Or was it their first objective, on featureless ground where all obvious landmarks had been destroyed? A short while later, Lyttelton heard the distinctive sound of a hunting horn and guessed correctly that it was Lieutenant Colonel John Campbell, commanding 2nd Coldstream. He was 'yelling "Stop!" and using some pretty expressive language to give it "tone"'. 'This is great fun,' said Lyttelton, to which Campbell responded: 'Fun be damned . . . We have taken everything in sight but, you blasted idiot, if you go on you will be in our own barrage. Don't you know this

Lieutenant Colonel John Campbell, VC

COLDSTREAM GUARDS

John Campbell was born in London in 1876 and commissioned into the Coldstream Guards in 1896, later serving in the South African War. He was awarded the VC for his actions while commanding 3rd Battalion Coldstream Guards at Ginchy on 15 September during the Battle of the Somme. His citation was published on 26 October 1916: 'For most conspicuous bravery and able leading in an attack. Seeing that the first waves of his battalion had been decimated by machine-gun fire and rifle fire he took personal command of the third line, rallied his men and with the utmost gallantry, and led them against the enemy machine-guns, capturing the guns and killing the personnel. Later in the day, after consultation with other unit commanders, he again rallied the survivors of his battalion, and at a critical moment led them through a very hostile fire barrage against the objective. He was the first to enter the enemy trench. His personal gallantry and initiative at a very critical moment turned the fortunes of the day and enabled the division to press on and captured objectives of the highest tactical importance.'

John Campbell was presented with his VC by the King at Buckingham Palace on 14 November 1916. In the same month he was appointed to command 137 Brigade in the temporary rank of Brigadier General. He retired from the Army in 1933 and during the Second World War commanded the 8th Battalion, Gloucestershire Home Guard. He died at Woodchester in Gloucestershire, aged 67, in 1944. His ashes were scattered on the River Findhorn in Scotland.

is the second objective? Dig! Where's my map? Where's my adjutant? Damn, he's been killed.'

But it was the first objective after all, a fact established by Campbell following a conference in a shell-hole. Once he knew where he was, he decided to push on, taking time to reorganise his 'mixed force' from 2nd Guards Brigade as best he could. Campbell had led his men magnificently throughout that morning. 2nd and 3rd Coldstream, advancing on the left, had been hit early on by machine-gun fire, losing most of the officers; the men hesitated, but Campbell rallied them with his hunting horn and the advance continued. The scene was later described by a Grenadier officer: 'Very few troops would have attemped to go against the tremendous fire, but the Coldstream, led by John Campbell, swung off their proper line, and went for the Boche like tigers, got into them with their bayonet, and killed every man of them.'

Above: *Lieutenant Colonel 'Crawley' de Crespigny, Commanding Officer, 2nd Battalion Grenadier Guards.*

Following up some 350 yards behind the two Coldstream battalions were 2nd Grenadiers, commanded by Lieutenant Colonel 'Crawley' de Crespigny, 'easily distinguished as he marched along, for he wore a forage cap in place of a helmet'. His men were advancing in 'artillery formation instead of in line', marching forward under the impression that they were to occupy positions already captured by the Coldstream. But the Germans were still there, in strength, and so getting into line for an attack that was in itself a costly manoeuvre. Somehow this was achieved and the enemy were driven back, thus strengthening the Guards Division's right flank.

One of de Crespigny's officer's was Harold Macmillan, who had been posted to 2nd Grenadiers in April, having recovered from his injuries at Loos while serving with 4th Battalion. He had received a second, relatively minor, wound in July 1916 while leading a patrol in no man's land, and was now back at the front. Advancing with his platoon on 15 September, he was struck by a shell fragment below his right kneecap but,

experiencing little pain, pushed on with his platoon. Then he received much more serious wounds at close range: machine-gun bullets into his pelvis and left thigh. He somehow managed to roll into a shell-hole where he remained for many hours. 'I had in my pocket Aeschylus's *Prometheus* in Greek. It was a play I knew very well, and seemed not inappropriate to my position . . . I read it intermittently.' He feigned dead to deceive a passing German patrol and waited to be rescued. 'My hole was twice blown in on top of me by shells exploding a few yards off. I was beginning now to feel the strain of waiting. I took ½ grain morphia, and succeeded in sleeping till 3:30pm.' At around 4pm, 'Company Sergeant-Major Norton, a splendid man, I can see him now . . . Bottom of shell-hole, sloped rifle: "Thank you, sir for leave to carry you away", as if he were on a parade ground.' Once back in Ginchy, Macmillan and another wounded officer, 'Dog' Ritchie, told their stretcher-bearers to return to the battalion while they looked for the field ambulance. At some stage in the darkness and confusion, the two officers became separated, and it was only then that Macmillan gave counsel to his fears: 'bravery is not really vanity, but a kind of concealed pride, because everybody is watching you. Then I was safe, but alone, and absolutely terrified because there was no need to show off any more, no need to pretend . . . there was nobody for whom you were responsible, not even the stretcher bearers'.

Somehow Macmillan made his way back, was picked up by a horse-drawn ambulance, and within a few days was back in hospital in England where, in a letter to his mother, he recorded his good luck. While he had received a bullet in his pelvis, it had passed through his water bottle and fortunately had not caused a fracture. The surgeons decided not to attempt a removal of the bullet; his wounds were dressed but not drained, allowing abscesses to form. Had it not been for

his mother's swift action in removing him to a private hospital in London, Macmillan believes he probably would have died. As it was, he spent the remainder of the war in and out of hospital, and this wound left him for the remainder of his life with 'a limp handshake, a dragging gait, and sporadic pain'.

Macmillan's war service clearly had a profound effect on him. As the military historian Brian Bond has observed,

> coming from a completely unmilitary background [he] was at first unsettled by unfamiliar routines and traditions, but in retrospect became tremendously proud of his service in the Grenadier Guards. He took genuine pleasure in the high standards of discipline, including the smartness and beauty of drill. The Guards' standard of excellence, he considered, provided a good working rule for civilian life.

He regarded service with the Brigade of Guards as 'the only tolerable form of soldiering, because they always had a view that if anything was done, it must be done as well as possible . . . I think it created in me a view of perfection, which I didn't have before.'

1st and 2nd Guards Brigades had fought their way to their second objective in the face of a determined enemy and against all odds. They had faced enfilade machine-gun fire from unexpected directions, had been forced to advance sometimes in the absence of the planned creeping barrage, and the new tanks that

Above: The Guards Divisional Canteen for the wounded at Guillemont, September 1916. Note the banner bearing the Guards Divisional Sign. The notice on the board read: 'For Wounded: Tea, Cake etc. Free at any hour'.

Above left: *Lieutenant Raymond Asquith, Grenadier Guards.*

had been promised in support played no part in this essentially infantry battle. The divisions advancing on either side of the Guards had experienced their own problems, and as a result the Guards found themselves exposed in a salient along the Fourth Army front and the time had now come for others to continue the advance. On 16 September, having resisted enemy attempts to recapture lost ground, 1st and 2nd Guards Brigades were withdrawn.

Two Guards VCs were awarded at Ginchy: one to Lieutenant Colonel John Campbell for his gallantry and leadership, and the other to Lance Sergeant Fred McNess, Scots Guards, who organised a counter-attack which he personally led, despite being severely wounded. On that same day, Raymond Asquith, serving with 3rd Grenadiers, was hit in the chest and later died on the way to the dressing station. An eyewitness described how 'in order to prevent his men from knowing the worst at once, he lit a cigarette after he fell, before being given morphia'. A private soldier, in a letter home, wrote that 'there is not one of us who would not have changed places with him if we had thought that he would have lived, for he was one of the finest men who ever wore the King's uniform, and he did not know what fear was'. Asquith was indeed an exceptional and talented man, described in a letter by Winston Churchill to his widow as 'my brilliant hero-friend'. Aged 37 when he died, Asquith was one of those who came to represent the 'doomed youth' of Wilfred Owen's poem. To quote his biographer, 'it was for what he was, rather than for what he did, that Raymond Asquith occupied a unique place in the admiration and affection of his generation'. Although he was the Prime Minister's son, his death brought no privilege or special treatment. Raymond Asquith is buried in Guillemont Road Cemetery, not far from where he died.

The Guards Division was back in the line three days after the fighting at Ginchy, following a short period of rest and reorganisation. Casualties had been heavy on the Somme, particularly among officers and non-commissioned officers. In the period 10–17 September, 54 officers and 598 other ranks had been killed with nearly 4,000 missing or wounded. But remarkably, these losses were quickly replaced since, to quote the official historian, the Guards Division always had a plentiful supply of men from home, 'imbued by their instructors with the methods, the tradition and the moral of the Brigade of Guards, fit and ready to take their places in the line'.

Lance Sergeant Fred McNess, VC
SCOTS GUARDS

Fred McNess was born in 1891, in Bramley, Yorkshire. He joined the Scots Guards in 1915, serving with the 3rd (Reserve) Battalion in London. In April 1916, now a Corporal, he was transferred to the 1st Battalion in France. In August 1916 he was promoted to Lance Sergeant. It was during the advance from Ginchy to Lesbœufs in September 1916 that Fred McNess took part in an action for which he was awarded the VC. His citation was published on 26 October 1916: 'For most conspicuous bravery. During a severe engagement, he led his men on with greatest dash in the face of heavy shell and machine-gun fire. When the first line of the enemy trenches was reached, it was found that the left flank was exposed and that the enemy were bombing the trench.

Sergeant McNess thereupon organised a counter-attack and led it in person. He was very severely wounded in the neck and jaw, but went on passing through the barrage of hostile bombs in order to bring up fresh supplies of bombs to his own men. Finally he established a "block" and continued encouraging his men and throwing bombs until utterly exhausted by loss of blood'.

He was evacuated back to a hospital in London, and on 9 December received his VC from the King at Buckingham Palace. He was discharged from the Army in June 1918 as 'No longer physically fit for war service'. Fred McNess committed suicide in April 1956; the injuries he received during the war had greatly affected him. He is buried in Bournemouth.

The Foot Guards' Bands at the Front

From the early days of mobilisation in and around London, the Foot Guards' bands played an important role, maintaining the morale of both soldiers and civilians. They performed in barracks, at railway stations, on Horse Guards Parade, in Trafalgar Square and elsewhere. But it took a little time for the War Office to realise that soldiers in the front line might also benefit from stirring military music as well as light-hearted entertainment such as parodies of popular German tunes. Bandsmen in the Line Infantry were serving along the Western Front as stretcher-bearers, but it was not until after the formation of the Guards Division in 1915 that the Guards bands began to visit the front line.

The first visit was by the Band of the Grenadier Guards under Captain Albert Williams in October 1915, becoming the only Guards band to receive the 1914–15 Star. The band played the National Anthem at Harfleur to coincide with one of the King's visits, and then joined the Guards Division at Sailly-Labourse. Over the next three months the band gave two or sometimes three performances a day to the soldiers, as well a concert in Paris in aid of the French Red Cross. In January 1916 the Coldstream Guards Band, under Captain John Mackenzie Rogan, took over. Captain Mackenzie Rogan, at 65 years of age, and thought to be the oldest man serving at the front, had the idea of playing to Guards battalions as they marched to and from the trenches. He recalled meeting 3rd Coldstream Guards en route to the front line: 'They, good chaps, were tramping along, each man carrying his seventy or eighty pounds of kit, and many of them bent over with the weight of it. But, at the first tap of the big drum the difference in those self-same men was wonderful to see, and when the band began to play there were cheers you might have heard miles away. It was a wondrous and very affecting experience. . .'

The Coldstream Band played for the Irish Guards on St Patrick's Day 1916 as they marched back towards the trenches. As Mackenzie Rogan recalled, 'We wheeled off at the parting

Far left: *Captain (later Major) Mackenzie Rogan.*

place and played them past to the tune of 'St. Patrick's Day'. The Colonel, as they went, cried out his thanks to us all. I prayed that the fine fellows might come back with as little loss as might be'. While playing for their own 1st Battalion, the band came under fire 'with earth-shaking shells exploding all the time a few hundred yards away from us and a big air fight proceeding simultaneously'. The Scots Guards band, under its bandmaster, Mr Fred Wood, arrived in May 1916, to be relieved three months later by the Band of the Irish Guards under Mr Charles Hassell. During the winter the band often played in the open in very cold conditions, as well as at the Irish Guards' Christmas dinner when the men each had a quarter pound of plum pudding, a quart of beer and two packets of cigarettes.

In May 1917 the Massed Bands, under their Senior Director of Music, Major John Mackenzie Rogan, visited Paris at the request of the French government. The bands wore full dress uniforms and were led by five drum majors in state dress and performed at various venues including the Tuileries, the Citroën munitions factory, and in hospitals. This successful visit to Paris led to an invitation to Italy in February 1918, during which the Pope asked to receive the Roman Catholic members of the bands at the Vatican and the bands later played at La Scala Opera House in Milan. The British Ambassador later wrote that 'No better propaganda work had been done for the Allied cause than the visit of the Guards Bands to Rome'.

During the last big German offensive launched on 21 March 1918 the Band of the Welsh Guards nearly lost their instruments when the Guards Division in Arras was redeployed at short notice. The Bandmaster, Mr Harris, and Sergeant Lumley returned for a search, became lost in the darkness close to the German lines, and sensibly waited until dawn, managing to get away with their recovered instruments. The Band of the Grenadier Guards was at the front on 21 August when the Guards Division began the final advance, on a night when the German bombing lasted many hours. Among the many casualties were three Grenadier musicians, one of whom was the solo clarinettist, a very fine musician who lost his arm.

The Guards bands played an important role throughout the war: at the front, as well as helping to maintain morale back home and amongst Britain's allies, a small but invaluable contribution that could so easily go unrecognised.

LESBŒUFS

After Ginchy, the next task for the Guards Division was to capture the village of Lesbœufs in a coordinated attack along the Morval–Lesbœufs–Gueudecourt line.

Lesbœufs lay in lower ground just over the 'lip' of the plateau over which the Ginchy attack had taken place, and with several spurs extending to the north-east that would complicate the advance. In drawing on lessons from previous battles, Major General Feilding emphasised the need for the attacking troops to be well forward at the beginning of the attack, with strong reserves posted not far behind. The operation would be supported by an intricate artillery plan, with a standing barrage onto the three main objectives, together with a creeping barrage which would fall 100 yards in front of the advancing troops at zero hour, moving forward at 50 yards a minute.

By the early hours of 25 September, 1st and 3rd Guards Brigades were in the front line, which ran north-west to south-east, crossing the Ginchy–Lesbœufs road where the Guards cemetery stands today. The weather was fine and clear, and the ground more favourable for the attack than at Ginchy ten days earlier. At 12.35pm, zero hour, the creeping barrage began and four Guards battalions (2nd Grenadiers and 1st Irish Guards on the left, 2nd Scots Guards and 4th Grenadiers on the right) began their advance in two waves. Almost immediately, they came under heavy enemy artillery. The Irish Guards captured their first objective relatively easily, but the Grenadiers were held up by wire in front of the German trenches. The 'coolness and devotion of duty on the part of the officers and the steadiness of the men' prevailed, as a way was cut through the wire entanglements and the Grenadiers captured their first objective 'at the point of the bayonet'. This phase had been completed in a matter of minutes, but with the loss of most of the officers, who were 'picked off' while the wire was being cut.

Notwithstanding this, in less than an hour, the leading battalions of 1st Guards Brigade were ready to continue the advance to the second objective, and punctually at 1.35pm they moved forward behind the 'creeping barrage'. Opposition here was comparatively light, and an hour later the attack on the third objective began. By 3.30pm, Lesbœufs had been taken, with the Guards firmly established on the eastern side. In the meantime, 3rd Guards Brigade had also advanced upon their objectives further to the north. The Scots Guards captured their first objective with few casualties, but the Grenadiers, on their left, came across a German intermediate trench that had somehow escaped the British barrage. Despite intensive machine-gun and rifle fire from this unexpected enemy position, causing many casualties, 4th Grenadiers 'pressed on, and made short work of the Germans . . . over 150 were killed there with the bayonet'.

By the evening of 25 September, 1st and 3rd Guards Brigades were firmly in their new positions, with all objectives captured. The enemy had fought fiercely, but were now demoralised by their failure on this sector, and with the sight of 'Germans hurrying away northward', there was a feeling that perhaps this was the moment for the breakthrough that had been promised before almost every battle. There was even a call from some of the commanding officers at the front for the cavalry to exploit their success, but it was not to be. The difficulty of pushing the cavalry forward, and on such a narrow front, rendered this no more than a pipe dream prompted by the momentary elation of those who had fought their way successfully across three strongly-held objectives.

These two battles fought on the Somme, at Ginchy and Lesbœufs, did much to enhance the reputation of the Guards Division. Ginchy had been particularly difficult, since the Guards had advanced with both

General Sir Ivor Maxse
COLDSTREAM GUARDS

Ivor Maxse commanded 18th (Eastern) Division, one of Kitchener's New Army divisions, at the Battle of the Somme. In training this inexperienced division, he encouraged initiative and independence of mind among junior officers and non-commissioned officers, the corollary being something he later called 'drilling for initiative' which relied upon thorough planning and training. 18th Division gained a reputation for being one of the best-trained divisions in the BEF, performing well during the Somme offensive. As a divisional and corps commander, Ivor Maxse applied all his experience as a colonial soldier, and was responsible for developing a philosophy that was the inspiration for what became known as 'Battle Drills', a cornerstone of the British Army's approach to warfare.

their flanks exposed to enfilade fire; soldiers expect to be engaged from their front, but not simultaneously from left and right as well. The Lesbœufs attack was less challenging, and also extremely well planned and coordinated. At every level and in an impressive way, the Guards Division had performed well.

The Battle of the Somme finally ended on 18 November, with a total of over 1 million casualties and more than 300,000 dead. The British had advanced about 6 miles in that period, along a frontage of 16 miles, and while this fell well short of any kind of tactical victory, there were some less tangible achievements that have taken much of the last century to be fully appreciated. The BEF had become battle-

hardened; no longer was it an army of amateurs and enthusiastic volunteers. Tactical lessons had been learned and, more importantly, were now being applied at every level. The Guards Division, in this respect, had a distinct advantage over the other divisions. Guardsmen commanded Guardsmen; the staffs were Guardsmen; and the supporting arms, such as the Artillery, Engineers and Service Corps, became part of this cohesive grouping where excellence, attention to detail, and never accepting anything but the best was part of an ingrained culture and *esprit de corps*. Analogies with the parade ground were often the means by which outsiders such as newspaper correspondents sought to explain this well-honed military machine. It was well tried, and it worked.

The Somme battles for the Germans had, arguably, an altogether more negative effect than they had on the British. The German casualty rate had taken a heavy toll on the last remnants of their peacetime professional officers and soldiers, and this had come at a time in the war when replacing these losses with willing volunteers was all but impossible. The Somme battles also prompted a fairly major reassessment for the Germans, and a determination to avoid such attritional battles in the future. They had suffered elsewhere, most notably at Verdun and on the Eastern Front. To that end, in March 1917, the Germans withdrew from the Somme, establishing themselves on a new, shorter and specially constructed line of defences further east: the Hindenburg Line. As the Germans withdrew they destroyed villages, poisoned the water supply, cratered the roads and crossroads, and placed many booby traps along the way. Closing up on the Germans, even when out of contact with the enemy, would not be easy.

1917

The Guards Division spent the winter of 1916–17 on the Somme. The period following the big battles was taken up first with training and then later with a range of tasks which included the repair of roads and the re-digging of shattered defences, together with the relatively routine business of holding the front line. The weather conditions were often grim, while the landscape itself bore all the scars of the fighting that had taken place here in 1916. On both sides of the front line it was the elements that became the real enemy: the rain and bitter cold, the snow, and always, even if under a thin layer of ice, the mud. The routine was 'two days in and two days out of the trenches' with the Guards Division holding a front line described as a series of posts or islands in the mud. Reliefs were often conducted in the open, and 'so terrible was the condition of the ground that men often had to be dug out'.

Then, around the middle of March 1917, the Germans began their withdrawal. It came as no surprise to the British, since they had known since the previous year that the Hindenburg Line was being constructed further to the east. The Guards, along their own front line, began to move forward cautiously, as the Germans conducted rearguard actions that combined artillery fire, snipers and booby traps. The BEF was now in uncharted territory.

But soon, the Guards Division was withdrawn from the line and given the task of repairing some of the shattered roads and railways destroyed in the Somme battles. It was exhausting work: the removal of mud, the digging of ditches, the filling of shell-holes, the clearance of rubble, and many other tasks. This was a job for all ranks: the GOC reminding commanding officers in an order issued in April 1917 'that it was an old-established custom in the Guards for officers to take off their coats and work with their men'.

A destroyed wood on the Somme battlefield, autumn 1916.

One Day of Crowded Life in the Trenches

(EXCLUSIVE OF HUNS, SHELLS OR BULLETS)

5pm. Arrival in trenches. Temper normal. Half an hour trying to appear interested while the outgoing officer explains to you the enormous amount of work he has done during his time there.

5.30pm. Outgoing officer departs. Half an hour spent commenting with your own officers on the utter and complete absence of any signs of work whatever having been done since you were there last.

6pm. Start your own work for the night.

6.15pm. Telephone operator reports he has got connection with Battalion Headquarters. (N.B. Life in the trenches has now started.)

6.45pm. First instalment of messages handed in to you.

No. 1. You will hold respirator and smoke helmet drills frequently during your tour. AAA ['Action And Acknowledge']. The signal for respirators to be put on will be two G's on the bugle. AAA. Adjutant.

No. 2. Report at once if you have a fully qualified Welsh miner in your company who can speak French and German. AAA. Age not under 18 years. Adjutant.

No. 3. All respirators will be immediately withdrawn. AAA. The signal for putting them on will be two blasts of the whistle, and not as per the last part of my message 1 of this date. Adjutant.

No. 4. A French aeroplane with slightly curved wings giving it the appearance of a German one is known to be in your vicinity. AAA. Use your discretion in accordance with Anti-Aircraft Regulations, para. I, Section 5. Adjutant.

No. 5. Report at once number of windows of smoke helmets broken since you have been in the trenches. AAA. The signal will now be two beats on a shell gong, and not as per my message 3 in correction of my message 1. Adjutant.

No. 6. Re my message No. 4, for the word 'French' read 'German' and for the word 'German' read 'French'. AAA. You will still use your discretion.

7.30pm. Messages dealt with. Dinner.

8.30pm. Arrival of C.O. Suggests politely that your men would be better employed doing some other kind of work. Assent enthusiastically. All working parties changed over to different work. Temper indifferent.

9pm to 2am. Answer telephone messages.

2.30am. Stand to arms. Walk round and survey the result of the night's work. Find the majority of it has been blown in by trench mortars in the early morning.

3.30am. Try and sleep.

4am. Woken up to receive the following messages:

No. 115. All smoke helmets are to be immediately marked with the date of issue. AAA. If no date is known, no date should be marked and the matter reported accordingly.

No. 116. R.E. require a working party from your company tomorrow from 6 am to 7 pm. AAA. Strength 150, with suitable proportion of N.C.Os. AAA. Otherwise your work is to be continued as usual. Adjutant.

Above: *Captain Guy Rasch, Grenadier Guards.*

5am. Woken up to send in 'Situation Report'.
Report 'Situation normal'.
8am. Breakfast.
9 to 11am. Scraping off mud in Oxford Street.
Removing bits of bacon in Bond Street. Reburying
Fritz, who owing to a night's rain has suddenly
appeared in Regent Street.
11.15am. Arrival of Brigade Staff. Orders given
for everything that has been dug out in the night
to be filled in and everything that has been filled
in to be dug out.
11.16am. Departure of Brigade Staff. Brain now in
state of coma. Feel nothing except a dull wonder. Rest
of day spent in eating chocolates, writing letters home
to children, and picking flowers off the bank. Final
message can remember receiving is about 12 noon:

No. 271. The Brigadier-General and Staff will shortly
be round your trenches. Adjutant.

Major Guy Rasch, DSO, Grenadier Guards
Household Brigade Magazine, 1923

Above: *Lieutenant R. D. Leigh-Pemberton, Grenadier Guards,
who served with the Royal Flying Corps and was awarded an
MC as a pilot.*

THE HOUSEHOLD BATTALION

There had been a slow realisation throughout the winter of 1915–16 and through much of the Somme battles that the cavalry had little or no real utility in the industrialised and attritional forms of warfare that were now prevailing. While there was still a desire to retain some of the mounted arm, there was clearly an imbalance in manpower with the infantry who had suffered such heavy casualties. An additional challenge for the Household Cavalry was that new recruits, of which there was a plentiful supply, were now outnumbering the supply of horses and, in any event, to be side-lined in an army consisting predominantly of infantry was not desirable. The idea of a Household Battalion now took shape, and on 30 August 1916, Major General Sir Francis Lloyd, GOC London District, wrote:

> I had an interview with The King yesterday about the proposed Household Infantry Battalion. He fully approves and it is his distinct wish that it be formed as quickly as possible from the three regiments; men to be mixed up, in four Companies, Officers to come equally from the three Regiments as we propose.

The new infantry unit, the Household Battalion, formed in September 1916 at Hyde Park Barracks under the wing of the Reserve Regiment of 1st Life Guards. Captain Wyndham Portal, who had served from 1908 to 1911, was appointed commanding officer and remained in command until the battalion was disbanded in early 1918. On formation, the strength was 28 officers and 900 men. Over the next 14 months, 84 officers were to serve with the battalion, of which 22 were commissioned directly, with the remainder coming from the three parent Household Cavalry regiments, the Foot Guards and Line Cavalry regiments. The rank and file, who were perhaps a little better educated than the average infantryman, were paid the slightly higher cavalry rate of pay, and wore cavalry service dress. The only difference was that they would not be learning to ride since they were now infantry soldiers. The Reserve Regiment at Combermere Barracks in Windsor was responsible for training new recruits, of which over 2,000 were sent to the front to replace the battalion's casualties.

The Household Battalion trained in Hyde Park and later moved to Richmond Park before departing for France in early November 1916 as part of 4th Division. On 8 December it moved into front-line trenches at Sailly Sailliesel in the Somme. During the following year, the battalion faced many ordeals. In April 1917, it took part in the attack on Fampoux, taking heavy casualties. Early in the following month the battalion was again in action, at Rœux, where the Germans were finally forced out of the village at bayonet point. The fighting at Fampoux and Rœux had taken a heavy toll: 9 officers killed and a total of nearly 500 casualties, more than half the original strength. However, the Household

Left: *Men of the Household Battalion pull handcarts piled with knapsacks and blankets in Richmond Park, Surrey, November 1916.*

Battalion's greatest and final challenge was yet to come, during the Third Battle of Ypres, in October 1917.

On 12 October, the Household Battalion took part in the attack on to the village of Poelcapelle. Lieutenant Colonel Portal realised the key to the battle for the village was the early capture of Requette Farm, his battalion's objective, so that he could pivot around it while supporting his right flank. At 5.30am, the battalion moved off, and had soon lost touch with the Royal West Kents to their right. By 6.50am and despite heavy enemy fire, the farm, which consisted of a 'broken down pill box', had been captured along with 4 machine guns and 26 men. But this proved to be vital ground for the Germans who were determined to recapture it. With casualties mounting and only three officers left alive, they managed to hang on until 3pm, by which time the farm was all but surrounded, and only then did this 'gallant little garrison consent to retire'.

The Household Battalion lost 400 men but were soon brought up to strength by the arrival of 500 reservists and were back in action in Bourlon Wood during the closing phases of the Battle of Cambrai.

Above: *Captain Wyndham Portal, Life Guards, later Commanding Officer of the Household Battalion.*

Above left: *Soldiers of the Household Battalion receiving musketry training in England.*

However, the task of maintaining numbers in the battalion as well as in the three parent regiments was becoming too much of a strain. The 1st and 2nd Life Guards and The Royal Horse Guards were now being converted to the 1st, 2nd and 3rd Guards Machine Gun Regiments and the demand on manpower was greater than ever. The Household Battalion was disbanded on 16 February 1918, and in his message of thanks to all ranks, signed on 26 December 1918, the King wrote: 'It is with feelings of sympathy and regret that I communicate this farewell order. Military policy, however, demanded the absorption of the Household Battalion into other Units of my Army'. He concluded by saying, 'You can rest assured that as an infantry battalion formed from The 1st and 2nd Life Guards and The Royal Horse Guards, you have added yet another chapter to the grand traditions of my Household Cavalry'. In its short life of some 14 months,

Second Lieutenant John Dunville, VC

1ST (ROYAL) DRAGOONS

John Dunville was born in Marylebone in 1896, and his family were from Holywood in County Down. On the outbreak of war, rather than go up to Trinity College, Cambridge, where he had a place, he joined the Army and was commissioned into the Fifth Reserve Regiment of Cavalry, later transferring to the 6th (Inniskilling) Dragoons. He went to France in June 1915, fought at the Battle of Loos and then transferred to the 1st (Royal) Dragoons in January 1916. Three months later he contracted trench fever, spending the remainder of the year in England before returning to France in December 1916.

John Dunville was awarded a VC for his actions on 24–25 June 1917 while serving with his regiment in the infantry role near Ephy in France. His citation was published on 31 July 1917: 'For most conspicuous bravery. When in charge of a party consisting of scouts and Royal Engineers engaged in the demolition of the enemy's wire, this officer displayed great gallantry and disregard of all personal danger. In order to ensure the absolute success of the work entrusted to him, 2nd Lt. Dunville placed himself between an NCO of the Royal Engineers and the enemy's fire, and thus protected, this NCO was enabled to complete a work of great importance. 2nd Lt Dunville, although severely wounded, continued to direct his men in the wire-cutting and general operations until the raid was successfully completed, thereby setting a magnificent example of courage, determination and devotion to duty, to all ranks under his command. This gallant officer has since succumbed to his wounds'.

John Dunville died early on 26 June 1917. He is buried at Villers-Faucon Communal Cemetery in France. In August 1917, his VC was presented to his father by King George V.

the Household Battalion had established a considerable reputation through many battles and engagements. The soldiers in the battalion had never served with their parent regiments, and yet somehow they had managed to emulate both the ethos and traditions of the Household Cavalry in an exemplary way.

The Household Battalion did not have a standard or colour during its short life, although a King's Colour was made for it in 1919 and lodged by Colonel Wyndham Portal the following year in Holy Trinity Church, Windsor, where it still hangs. Although the Household Battalion was entitled to its own battle honours, Colonel Portal decided that these should be given to the three parent regiments of the Household Cavalry. So it was that the Household Battalion's colour bears no battle honours, since these are now embroidered on the standards of the Household Cavalry: *Ypres 1917, Scarpe 1917, Broodseinde, Poelcappelle* and *Passchendaele.*

Right: *The Guards marching through Cassel in Flanders en route to the Ypres Salient, 1917.*

Below: *The Battle of Pilckem Ridge. Three Irish Guardsmen wearing German body armour while examining a captured German machine gun, Pilckem, 31 July 1917.*

THE THIRD
BATTLE OF YPRES

In June 1917, the Guards Division was back in Flanders. During the Battle of Messines, which began on 7 June with the simultaneous and gigantic explosion of 20 mines along the German front line, the divisional artillery was in support, playing a useful role in this highly successful battle in which advances were made along the line in preparation for a larger attack in July. The Guards Trench Mortar Batteries also took part, helping to destroy wire in front of the German trenches.

On 10 June, Major General Feilding held a divisional conference to explain the forthcoming tasks for the Guards during the main offensive. The division was now moving into the Boesinghe sector, in the low-lying ground close to the Yser Canal and the village of Boesinghe. The canal, with a surface of about 70 feet of soft mud, lay in no man's land between the two front lines, and the ground beyond the German positions was flat and open for about 1,000 yards leading up to the higher ground and Houthulst Forest. To the north-west was Pilckem Ridge, the high ground held by the Germans from which they had a good view of the British trenches along the canal and also the communication system to the rear. As the official historian describes it, 'the position of the Guards was not a happy one from which to launch an offensive'. Not only would the Germans be able to observe preparations prior to the attack, but the canal was also a formidable obstacle, 'so formidable indeed, that neither side had made any serious attempt to cross it during the war'.

Crossing the Yser Canal swiftly was the key, and a number of solutions were considered, the most practical being offered by the Belgians. Canvas mats, about a yard in width and longer than the canal at its broadest point, were constructed with a reinforced backing of

Private Thomas Whitham, VC
COLDSTREAM GUARDS

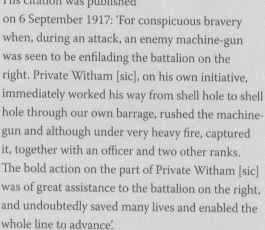

Thomas Whitham was born in 1888 near Burnley, Lancashire. He enlisted in the Coldstream Guards in January 1915, serving with the 5th Battalion until posted to the 1st Battalion in France in October. Thomas Whitham was awarded a VC for his action on 31 July 1917 at Pilckem, near Ypres, Belgium, during the Third Battle of Ypres. His citation was published on 6 September 1917: 'For conspicuous bravery when, during an attack, an enemy machine-gun was seen to be enfilading the battalion on the right. Private Witham [sic], on his own initiative, immediately worked his way from shell hole to shell hole through our own barrage, rushed the machine-gun and although under very heavy fire, captured it, together with an officer and two other ranks. The bold action on the part of Private Witham [sic] was of great assistance to the battalion on the right, and undoubtedly saved many lives and enabled the whole line to advance'.

Thomas Whitham received his VC from the King at Buckingham Palace on 19 October 1917. Thereafter, he remained in England, and was discharged from the Army in March 1918. He became a bricklayer for a while, but later had difficulties finding work, and was forced to pawn his VC. In October 1924, while looking for work, he received a severe head injury riding his bicycle, lost his memory, and was reported missing by his wife. He recovered, and briefly found work, but then died a few weeks later in the Royal Infirmary, Oldham. He is buried in Nelson, Lancashire.

wire netting and small wooden slats. A mat could be carried and rolled out by two men with relative ease, and by trialling on the Poperinghe Canal, it was proved that even if the mats sunk just below the waterline, they were usable with a rope handrail to indicate the line of the crossing point. But these mats could not be entirely relied upon if the level of water in the canal were to rise, and so some light, single-file, wooden

Sergeant Robert Bye, VC

WELSH GUARDS

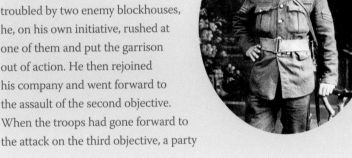

Robert Bye was born in Pontypridd, Glamorganshire in 1889. He worked for a while in a coal mine, and enlisted in the Army in 1915, serving with the Welsh Guards. He was promoted twice during 1916, and in April became a sergeant. He was awarded a VC for an action on 31 July 1917 close to Pilckem, near Ypres, Belgium, during the Third Battle of Ypres. His citation was published on 4 September 1917: 'For most conspicuous bravery. Sergeant Bye displayed the utmost courage and devotion to duty during an attack on the enemy's position. Seeing that the leading waves were being troubled by two enemy blockhouses, he, on his own initiative, rushed at one of them and put the garrison out of action. He then rejoined his company and went forward to the assault of the second objective. When the troops had gone forward to the attack on the third objective, a party was detailed to clear up a line of blockhouses which had been passed. Sergeant Bye volunteered to take charge of this party, accomplished his object, and took many prisoners. He subsequently advanced to the third objective, capturing a number of prisoners, thus rendering invaluable assistance to the assaulting companies. He displayed throughout the most remarkable initiative'.

He was discharged from the Welsh Guards, but had soon re-enlisted in the Nottinghamshire and Derbyshire Regiment. He left the Army in 1925, returned to the coalmines, and re-enlisted in the Sherwood Foresters during the Second World War. Robert Bye died in 1962 and is buried in Warsop, Nottinghamshire.

bridges were constructed by the Royal Engineers and mounted on empty petrol cans to provide buoyancy.

The Guards Division conducted a series of raids along their sector, some on a large scale. On the night of 19–20 July, the length of the enemy front was raided by 2nd Irish Guards on the left and 4th Grenadiers on the right. Mats were laid across the canal by 4th Coldstream, a Pioneer battalion, but rising water made these only partially successful, and some of the Irish Guardsmen on the right found themselves in water above their chests. When the Guards reached the enemy trenches, some had been abandoned, while the Grenadiers had a 'stiff fight' getting to their trenches, leading to a withdrawal under the covering fire of 4th Coldstream.

The main crossing of the canal came on 27 July following a report to the Divisional HQ indicating that there were few Germans in their sector. Based on this information, Major General Feilding decided to conduct the crossing in daylight, with no preliminary artillery support, to maximise surprise. He gave the task to 3rd Coldstream, and during the course of the day patrols were able to establish a temporary line some 1,000 yards

Lance Sergeant John Moyney, VC

IRISH GUARDS

John 'Jack' Moyney was born in 1895 in Rathdowney, Ireland, and worked for a while as a labourer before enlisting in the Irish Guards in April 1915. He served in England until October 1915 when he was posted to France. He was promoted twice during the following year, before becoming a lance sergeant (unpaid) in September 1916. Lance Sergeant Moyney was awarded a VC for the action that took place on 12–13 September 1917, at Broembeek, Belgium, during which another Irish Guardsman, Thomas Woodcock, was similarly awarded. Jack Moyney's citation was published on 17 September 1917: 'For most conspicuous bravery when in command of fifteen men forming two advanced posts. In spite of being surrounded by the enemy he held his post for 96 hours, having no water and little food. On the morning of the fifth day a large force of the enemy advanced to dislodge him. He ordered his men out of their shell holes, and, taking the initiative, attacked the advancing enemy with bombs, while he used his Lewis gun with great effect from a flank. Finding himself surrounded by superior numbers, he led back his men in a charge through the enemy, and reached a stream which lay between the posts and the line. Here he instructed his party to cross at once while he and Private Woodcock remained to cover their retirement. When the whole of his force had gained the south-west bank unscathed he himself crossed under a shower of bombs. It was due to endurance, skill and devotion to duty shown by this non-commissioned officer that he was able to bring his entire force safely out of action'.

John Moyney was discharged from the Army in 1919 and found a job with the railways back in Ireland. In 1977 he told a reporter that he had joined the Army 'for the heck of it and to see a bit of the world. There were posters going around encouraging people to join up. Some of the big employers were offering half wages to anyone who enlisted and the clergy were encouraging it off the altar'. Jack Moyney died in 1980. He is buried in Roscrea, County Tipperary.

beyond the canal, ideally placed for the main attack that was to follows three days later.

The attack began at 3.50am on 31 July behind a creeping barrage. By 10am all the Guards' objectives had been captured, and the enemy pushed back some 2½ miles along a frontage of 1,500 yards. That evening the rain began and the conditions became appalling.

'The men were standing up to their knees in water. Every shell-hole was a pond, and the going had become terrible'. Two VCs were won that day: by Thomas Whitham, Coldstream Guards, and Robert Bye, Welsh Guards. On 2 August, General Sir Hubert Gough congratulated Fifth Army for a highly successful operation. The enemy, he said, had been driven back by 'a front of about 8 miles'

with British and French troops 'firmly established in or beyond the German second line on a front of 7 miles'. Although the Third Battle of Ypres was to continue for another three months, much of the Allies' success was achieved in those opening weeks; now it was a case of consolidating and hanging on to these gains in the appalling conditions of the Flanders mud.

On 27 August, the Guards battalions were back in the new front line, now further to the north-east towards Broembeek stream at Ney crossroads. The next task was the crossing of this stream. Major General Feilding

Private Thomas Woodcock, VC

IRISH GUARDS

Thomas Woodcock was born in 1888 in Wigan, Lancashire. On leaving school, he became a miner, and although in this occupation he was exempted from service, he enlisted in May 1915. He was later posted to 2nd Battalion Irish Guards and was sent to France in December 1915. The citation for his VC was published on 17 September 1917: 'For most conspicuous bravery and determination. He was one of a post commanded by Lance Sergeant Moyney which was surrounded. The post held out for 96 hours, but after that time was attacked from all sides in overwhelming numbers and was forced to retire. Private Woodcock covered the retirement with a Lewis gun, and only retired when the enemy had moved round and up to his post and were only a few yards away. He then crossed the river, but hearing cries for help behind him, returned and waded into the stream amid a shower of bombs from the enemy and rescued another member of the party. The latter he then carried across the open ground in broad daylight towards our front line regardless of machine gun fire that was opened on him'.

Thomas Woodcock remained in France until March 1918, when he returned to his home town of Wigan where he was welcomed by a civic reception. He returned to France a few weeks later and was killed in action on 27 March 1918. He is buried in the British Cemetery at Douchy-les-Ayette, France.

Lance Sergeant John Rhodes, VC, DCM & BAR
GRENADIER GUARDS

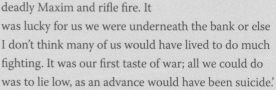

John Rhodes was born in 1891 in Packmoor, Staffordshire, and after school worked at Chatterley Whitfield Colliery. He enlisted in the Grenadier Guards in 1911, serving for three years with the 3rd Battalion in London, Pirbright and Aldershot. In 1913 he transferred to the reserve, and was recalled on the outbreak of war. He was posted to 2nd Battalion Grenadier Guards in August, leaving for France shortly after. Describing the retreat from Mons in a letter home, he wrote: 'When we got to the base of the bank we were met with a deadly Maxim and rifle fire. It was lucky for us we were underneath the bank or else I don't think many of us would have lived to do much fighting. It was our first taste of war; all we could do was to lie low, as an advance would have been suicide.'

In January 1915 Rhodes was promoted to Lance Corporal, and on 18 May, at Rue du Bois, near Armentières, he conducted a patrol from which he returned with some valuable information about the enemy. He twice went out under heavy fire to bring back wounded men, and for his bravery was awarded the DCM. During an action on 6 August 1915 at Givenchy, Rhodes and Private Barton ran forward to rescue men who had been buried when several saps in the front-line trench had collapsed due to enemy fire. For their bravery Barton was awarded the DCM and Rhodes was given a bar to his DCM. Rhodes was wounded in the shoulder and evacuated to England, where he was posted to the 5th (Reserve) Battalion, later being promoted to Lance Sergeant. Following his recovery, he was posted to 3rd Battalion in France in early 1917.

John Rhodes' VC was awarded for his action at Houthulst Forest, Belgium, on 9 October 1917. The citation for his VC was published on 26 November 1917: 'For most conspicuous bravery when in charge of a Lewis gun section covering the consolidation of the right front company.

He accounted for several enemy with his rifle as well as by Lewis gun fire and, upon seeing three enemy leave a "pill-box", he went out single-handed through our own barrage and hostile machine-gun fire, and effected an entry into the "pill-box." He there captured nine enemy, including a forward observation officer connected by telephone with his [artillery] battery. These prisoners he brought back with him, together with valuable information'.

John Rhodes was seriously wounded the day after his VC had been gazetted. Carroll Carstairs, an American serving with the Grenadiers, saw him being carried into the Clearing Station: 'He was a fine big man, but lying deep in the stretcher and covered with a blanket, he seems immeasurably to have shrunk . . . . all his great strength and courage is ebbing fast'. He died shortly afterwards, while back home that day the news of his VC had just reached his family. His Commanding Officer, Lieutenant Colonel Andrew Thorne, DSO, later wrote to his wife Elizabeth: 'I am afraid he never knew that he had got his VC. He was wounded on the morning of the 27 November and died as he reached the casualty clearing station. We called there to tell him but it was too late'.

John Rhodes was buried at the Rocquigny-Equancourt Road British Cemetery, Manancourt, on the Somme. His widow was unable to come to Buckingham Palace to receive the medal; it was presented to her at her home in Tunstall on 15 July 1918 by an officer from a local barracks.

had hoped that this might be achieved by stealth, but in the event the German presence there was stronger, requiring a full-scale assault. This attack would have certainly been carried out had it not been for the unexpected actions of the enemy, who launched surprise attacks on the British outposts in Ney Wood on 10 September. It was in the fighting that followed that two further VCs were won: by John Moyney and Thomas Woodcock, both Irish Guards.

Above: *Two bombers and bayonet men at the end of a sap occupied by Left Flank, 2nd Scots Guards during an attack on 17 October 1915. During this attack 5 officers and 110 other ranks were killed or wounded.*

THE BATTLE OF CAMBRAI

By early November, the Guards Division had moved south again, to the sector east of the old Somme battlefields, in preparation for the offensive towards Cambrai. Much was expected here, the aim being to break through the Hindenburg Line with the support of tanks on a large scale and without the long preliminary artillery bombardment of previous offensives. The prize was the high ground just to the north of Cambrai, together with a deceptively large and dominating feature: Bourlon Wood.

The battle began at dawn on 20 November, with a bombardment on the German defences followed by smoke and a creeping barrage to protect the advance of six infantry divisions, supported by over 300 tanks. There was some early success, with the Hindenburg Line breached and Ribécourt and Marcoing captured.

Below: *A British tank crossing a trench prior to the Battle of Cambrai, November 1917.*

Below right: *Lieutenant General Sir Francis Lloyd, GOC London District, inspecting a British tank taking part in the Lord Mayor's Show, London, 9 November 1917.*

The British had advanced some 5 miles, a great achievement in one day given the ghastly attrition of the Somme battles the previous year. It seemed that the British were about to achieve one of the great victories of the war so far. Back home, the church bells rang for the first time since 1914.

Haig was determined to take Bourlon Ridge. The exhausted 62nd Division was replaced by 40th Division, commanded by Major General John Ponsonby, a Coldstream Guardsman who had commanded 2nd Guards Brigade. Well supported by tanks and artillery, 40th Division attacked Bourlon Ridge on 23 November but with little success. The ridge had now been reinforced by two German divisions with more in reserve. Although 40th Division reached the crest, it suffered huge casualties.

The Guards Division had been ordered forward on 21 November and now with 62nd Division was given the order to capture Bourlon Wood and the village of Fontaine-Notre-Dame. The attack began at 6.20am on 27 November, with the Guards Division (2nd Guards

Above: *Wreckage of British tanks at Bourlon Wood, c.1917.*

Left: *A view across a battle-scarred landscape around Bourlon Wood, 1918.*

Brigade) on the left and the 62nd Division on the right, advancing behind a creeping barrage.

Around midnight on 26 September, Harold Alexander, now in command of 2nd Irish Guards, gave orders to his company commanders for the attack at dawn into Bourlon Wood, on the high ground that overlooks the western approaches to Cambrai. Alexander's brother William, a company commander in the battalion, described the scene:

It was bitterly cold and snowing hard. We formed up in dense undergrowth. The attack never looked like anything except a failure. The barrage was thin, and advanced too quick. The Germans retaliated strongly. We captured four hundred prisoners in the wood, but two hundred of them escaped by attacking their guards, or when the escorts were killed by shelling. Then the enemy counter-attacked round our left flank, and the Battalion was almost surrounded. The state of things in and around the chalet where Battalion H.Q. was located cannot be adequately described. There was no place for a dressing station. Near all the orderlies were killed or wounded. The whole place was stacked with dead, dying and wounded, and it is no exaggeration to say that the floor of the chalet was running with blood, and still

Sergeant John McAulay, VC, DCM

SCOTS GUARDS

John McAulay was born in 1888 in Kinghorn, Fife. Following school, he joined the Glasgow Police and then enlisted in the Scots Guards on 4 September 1914, serving with 3rd (Reserve) Battalion in London before being posted to 1st Battalion in France on 5 January 1915, where he was later promoted to sergeant.

On 25 June 1917 McAulay and his platoon were ordered to conduct a reconnaissance of the Yper Lea stream. When the platoon commander was killed, McAulay not only assumed command, but also cleared two strongly-held dugouts, killing all the occupants, several of them single-handedly. For this action, Sergeant McAulay was later awarded the DCM.

On 27 November 1917, during the Battle of Cambrai, Sergeant McAulay took part in an action for which he was awarded the VC. His citation was published in the *London Gazette* on 11 January 1918: 'For most conspicuous bravery and initiative in attack. When all his officers had become casualties Sergeant McAulay assumed command of the company and under shell and machine-gun fire successfully held and consolidated the objective gained. He reorganised the company, cheered on and encouraged his men, and under heavy fire at close quarters showed utter disregard of danger. Noticing a counter-attack developing on his exposed left flank, he successfully repulsed it by the skilful and bold use of machine-guns, aided by two men only, causing heavy enemy casualties. Sergeant McAulay also carried his company commander, who was mortally wounded, a long distance to a place of safety under very heavy fire.

Twice he was knocked down by the concussion of a bursting shell, but, undaunted, he continued on his way until his objective was achieved, killing two of the enemy who endeavoured to intercept him. Throughout the day this very gallant non-commissioned officer displayed the highest courage, tactical skill, and coolness under exceptionally trying circumstances.'

John McAulay was briefly an acting Company Sergeant Major in April 1918. He left the Army in early 1919, returning to the Glasgow Police where, in 1922, he was promoted to Inspector. He died on 14 January 1956, and is buried in Glasgow.

Above: *Major General John Ponsonby, Coldstream Guards.*

Above right: *Major (later Lieutenant Colonel) the Honourable Harold Alexander, Irish Guards.*

this merciless shelling continued, aided by low-flying aeroplanes. In the midst of this pandemonium an orderly rushed in to say that the Germans had broken through and were streaming down the wood, and were even now behind Battalion H.Q.

Where thousands would have given up in despair, there was one man who stood head and shoulders above everyone else. The Commanding Officer [Harold Alexander], calm, cool, and collected, never lost his head for one moment, but seemed to affect everyone with his courage, steadiness and determination. We all looked to him for support, having absolute confidence in his skill and foresight.

Of the 400 Irish Guardsmen that Alexander had led into the wood that day, 80 were to return. 'Alex' had displayed a remarkable style of leadership, a strength of character and utter coolness that seemed to transcend the situation around him. His qualities as a Guardsman and commander were to serve him well, for this was the same man who would become a senior Allied commander in the next war and Winston Churchill's model of a perfect general.

The Germans' counter-attack came early on the morning of 30 November, with the combined efforts of three British divisions just about holding the line in front of Bourlon Wood, but the situation remained critical. Over the next few hours, orders changed on several occasions, and it was only around midday that clear plans emerged. Receiving orders from above to occupy the high ground east of Gouzeaucourt, Brigadier General 'Crawley' de Crespigny, commanding 1st Guards Brigade,

Captain George Paton, VC, MC

GRENADIER GUARDS

George Paton was born on 3 October 1895 at Innellan, Argyleshire. He was commissioned into the 2nd Battalion, 17th County of London Regiment in October 1914, transferring to the Grenadier Guards two years later. He was awarded an MC following an action at Boesinghe in Belgium in which, despite a heavy barrage, he led his company 'with splendid initiative and sound military judgement'. Four months later, he was awarded a VC for an action that took place at Gonnelieu, France, on 1 December 1917. His citation was published in the *London Gazette* on 13 February 1918:

'For most conspicuous bravery and self-sacrifice. When a unit on his left was driven back, thus leaving his flank in the air and his company practically surrounded, he fearlessly exposed himself to re-adjust the line, walking up and down within fifty yards of the enemy under a withering fire. He personally removed several wounded men, and was the last to leave the village. Later, he again re-adjusted the line, exposing himself regardless of all danger the whole time, and when the enemy four times counterattacked he sprang each time upon the parapet, deliberately risking his life, and being eventually mortally wounded, in order to stimulate his command. After the enemy had broken through on his left, he again mounted the parapet, and with a few men—who were inspired by his great example—forced them once more to withdraw, thereby undoubtedly saving the left flank.'

George Paton is buried at the Metz-en-Couture Communal Cemetery (British Extension), in France. His VC and MC were presented to his parents by the King on 2 March 1918.

rode forward with his commanding officers as soldiers from other units, 'many of them without their rifles and equipment, were streaming westward across country in a state of great disorder'. It seemed that the enemy had captured Gouzeaucourt and was poised to advance. De Crespigny decided to launch an immediate counter-attack, with 2nd and 3rd Coldstream attacking from the south, 1st Irish Guards assaulting from the north, and 2nd Grenadiers in reserve.

The three battalions came down into Gouzeaucourt together under heavy machine-gun fire. Somehow they managed to keep going, sweeping through the village, making their way up the slope to the east. By 1.30pm, Gouzeaucourt was secure, and some 100 prisoners had been captured. It had been a successful operation, well supported by the Guards machine-gun sections moving with the battalions. Following this, the remaining two brigades moved forward to join 1st Guards Brigade, as the division prepared for the next attack on to the Quentin Ridge and Gauche Wood, supported by tanks.

Zero hour was 6.20am the following morning, and while some of the assigned tanks made it to the start line, taking up the advance in front of the infantry, 2nd Grenadiers had no option but to go on alone. Somehow they made it into the wood, overpowering some of the enemy machine-gunners. The tanks had all been stopped by artillery fire, but some of their crews had managed to get forward and support the Grenadiers with their Lewis guns. In the meantime, 3rd Coldstream, led by four tanks, captured the Quentin Ridge, and from there were able to support the 3rd Guards Brigade's attack on to Gonnelieu.

The attack on Gonnelieu began at 6.20am on 1 December 1917, with 1st Welsh Guards on the right and 4th Grenadiers on the left. The Welsh Guards with one tank in support managed to push forward to the high ground south-west of Gonnelieu in the face of stiff resistance. The Grenadiers, with no tank support, were less fortunate, taking extremely heavy casualties. The capture of Gonnelieu was beyond their reach, and the Commanding Officer, Viscount Gort, decided to establish a defensive position outside the village. In the process of achieving this, Gort was severely wounded and had to be evacuated.

Although Gonnelieu had not been captured, the overall effect of the Guards Division's capturing of Gouzeaucourt and the high ground to the east had stabilised the front and brought the German counter-attack to an end. Sir Douglas Haig was full of praise, as was Lieutenant General Sir William Pulteney, the Scots Guardsman in command of III Corps, expressing his

appreciation of the prompt manner in which [the Guards Division] turned out on 30 November, counter-attacked through a disorganised rabble and retook Gouzeaucourt. This very fine attack which was subsequently carried against Quentin ridge and Gauche Wood, resulting in the capture of these important positions, was worthy of the highest traditions of the Guards.

Above: *Lieutenant General Sir William Pulteney, Scots Guards. 'Putty', as he was known, commanded III Corps from 1914 to 1918, and was one of the longest-serving corps commanders of the war.*

The Battle of Cambrai ended on 3 December. Within a few days, most of the British gains had been abandoned in the face of fierce German counter-attacks and, had it not been for the success of the Guards Division attacks

around Gouzeaucourt, the situation would have been much worse. The progress in the early stages of the battle, with the use of tanks, coordinated with infantry, artillery and aeroplanes, had engendered hope at the front and stirred the spirit back home. Perhaps the key to attacks against strong defences had been found, but the Germans had also learnt lessons; their swift counter-attacks and new storm trooper tactics had given them an advantage that, on this occasion, the British could not match.

Casualties on both sides were around 40,000, a high figure given that the battle lasted for just two weeks. The Guards Division's casualties were over 3,000 and, critically, the losses among instructors and trained soldiers had been particularly heavy. The two attacks in which they had participated had been launched at short notice, in a general state of confusion and near panic, without much artillery support, and against a determined enemy fighting from good defensive positions.

Above top: *Internees at Murren, Switzerland, 4 December 1917. Left to right: Trooper Ormiston, The Life Guards, Corporal Taylor, Grenadier Guards, Private Speight, Scots Guards, Private, Welsh Guards (unknown), Private Walsh, Irish Guards, Private, Coldstream Guards (unknown).*

Above: *Members of a German storm trooper unit.*

The Irish Guards in Bourlon Wood

RUDYARD KIPLING

In honour of his lost son, Kipling compiled and edited the two volumes of The Irish Guards in the Great War, *which many believe contain some of his finest writing:* 'In some respects Bourlon was like Villers-Cotterêts on a large scale, with the added handicap of severe and well-placed shelling. A man once down in the coppice, or bogged in a wood-pool, was as good as lost, and the in-and-out work through the trees and stumpage broke up the formations. Nor, when the affair was well launched, was there much help from "the officer with the compass" who was supposed to direct the outer flank of each company. The ground on the right of the Battalion's attack, which the Coldstream were handling, was thick with undestroyed houses and buildings of all sorts that gave perfect shelter to the machine-guns; but it is questionable whether Bourlon Wood itself, in its lack of points to concentrate upon, and in the confusion of forest rides all exactly like each other, was not, after all, the worst. Early in the advance, No. 2 Company lost touch on the left, while the rest of the Battalion, which was still somehow keeping together, managed to get forward through the Wood as far as its north-east corner, where they made touch with the 1st Coldstream. Not long after this, they tried to dig in among the wet tree-roots, just beyond the Wood's north edge. It seemed to them that the enemy had fallen back to the railway line which skirted it, as well as to the north of La Fontaine village. Officially, the objective was reached, but our attacking strength had been used up, and there were no reserves. A barrage of big stuff, supplemented by field-guns, was steadily threshing out the centre and north of the Wood, and, somewhere to the rear of the Battalion a nest of machine-guns broke out viciously and unexpectedly. Then the whole fabric of the fight appeared to crumble, as, through one or other of the many gaps between the Battalions, the enemy thrust in, and the 2nd Irish Guards, hanging on to their thin front line, realized him suddenly at their backs. What remained of them split up into little fighting groups; sometimes taking prisoners, sometimes themselves being taken, and again breaking away from their captors, dodging, turning, and ducking in dripping coppices and over the slippery soil, while the shells impartially smote both parties. Such as had kept their sense of direction headed back by twos and threes to their original starting-point; but at noon Battalion Headquarters had lost all touch of the Battalion, and the patrols that got forward to investigate reported there was no sign of it. It looked like complete and unqualified disaster. But men say that the very blindness of the ground hid this fact to a certain extent both from us and the enemy . . . . As one man said: "If Jerry had only shut off his dam' guns and *listened* he'd ha' heard we was knocked out; but he kept on hammer-hammering an' rushin' his parties back and forth the Wood, and so, ye see, them that could of us, slipped back quiet in the height of the noise." Another observer compared it to the chopping of many foxes in cover—not pleasant, but diversified by some hideously comic incidents. All agreed that it was defeat for the Guards—the first complete one they had sustained.'

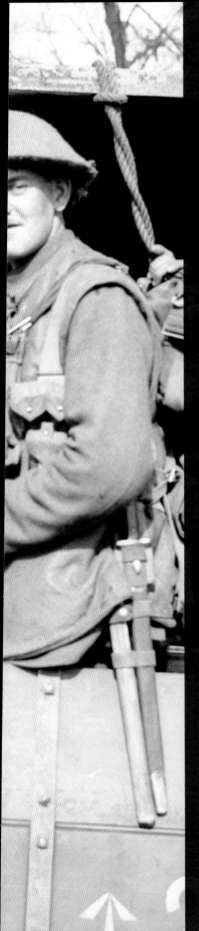

1918

THE GUARDS DIVISION MOVED TO THE ARRAS SECTOR IN DECEMBER 1917 as the war on the Eastern Front ended and the Germans began to move divisions to France and Flanders. The BEF had a manpower crisis in early 1918, with many line battalions, but not the Guards, being disbanded to bring others up to strength. In February 1918 4th Guards Brigade was re-formed with 4th Grenadiers, 3rd Coldstream, and 2nd Irish Guards, and placed under command of 31st Division.

The German offensive began on 21 March, with huge gains along the line and over 20,000 British troops taken on that day. This was the Germans' last chance of a swift victory before the Americans arrived, and they had made an impressive start. The Allies faced the possibility of defeat as, on 11 April, Haig issued his famous 'backs to the wall' order. 4th Guards Brigade was despatched to Hazebrouck, just 30 miles from Calais, to block a gap in the line. Oliver Lyttelton, the Brigade Major, recalled the Corps Commander pointing to a large map at Corps HQ: 'Between these two points there are no British troops. The best German corps on this front is pressing through this gap and, gentlemen, unless you do something before morning there'll be no more fox-hunting. Good evening gentlemen'. The task was to hold the line until Australian reinforcements arrived.

Late on 11 April, 4th Guards Brigade took up its positions along an ill-defined line. The ground was flat, with drainage ditches and hardly any cover, and a shortage of spades left the soldiers badly exposed at dawn. There was no information about flanking units or the enemy, and to make matters worse, there was no food.

Soldiers of 2nd Grenadiers near Arras, 22 March 1918.

HAZEBROUCK

The Germans attacked on 12 April, with the Northumberland Fusiliers holding them at bay until 9am. The Brigade Commander, Brigadier General Butler, now had a difficult decision: stay in the gap or move forward to hold the open flank. He decided on the latter and the Grenadiers and Coldstream advanced to the south-east with the Irish Guards protecting their right flank. Rudyard Kipling later described the Irish Guards 'working to word and whistle ("like sporting-dog trials") under and among the shrapnel, whizz-bangs that trundled along the ground, bursts of machine-gun fire and stray sniping', but still they pushed on. The advance failed with heavy casualties and one Coldstream company was down to 40 men under the command of Sergeant Vickers, but somehow successive German attacks were halted. That night was spent in the open, as there were no trenches, just a number of strongpoints held by a few men. No one knew precisely where they were, ammunition was low, and everyone was tired.

The Germans attacked again in the morning; some Coldstream positions were captured, but the depleted No. 1 Company was still delaying the Germans with Sergeant Vickers now sending crisp messages to the Commanding Officer from 'OC No.1 Coy'. The previous night he reported 'Situation normal . . . Map reference not known. No map' before giving a brief account of the earlier fighting and casualties. His message on 13 April was equally succinct, noting his flanking units and the extent of his frontage.

Soon, a German breakthrough on the northern flank left a Grenadier company surrounded close to Vieux-Berquin. Captain Thomas Pryce now sent his last message, 'My left flank is entirely in the air . . . . Enemy advancing'. By that evening, with no ammunition and only a few men, Pryce gave the order to charge with fixed bayonets that knocked the Germans back, but then they attacked again. Thomas Pryce was killed leading his men, and later awarded a VC. One soldier made it back across the lines that night, and 14 were taken prisoner. The Germans had lost momentum, the Australians were firmly in place, and the battle was over. The actions of 4th Guards Brigade at Hazebrouck were not recorded in the Guards Division's official history because the brigade was serving in another division. During this 'forgotten battle' a much larger German force had been stopped, Hazebrouck was saved, and a breakthrough to the coast some 30 miles away had been prevented. During three days of battle 4th Guards Brigade (including 12th King's Own Yorkshire Light Infantry) lost a total 425 killed, 606 wounded, and 469 taken prisoner. As Frederick Ponsonby later wrote: 'Orders were issued . . . that every position was to be held to the last man. The 4th Guards Brigade . . . displayed the most heroic courage and tenacity in successfully holding back large numbers of the enemy . . . [the battalions now] practically annihilated, the dogged resistance of the survivors led the Germans to imagine they were being opposed by superior numbers'.

By July the German momentum was faltering as supply lines were extended and casualties mounted. On 8 August the British launched the Battle of Amiens, marking the last phase of the war. On 21 August the Guards Division was back in action, with all three brigades involved in attacks towards Saint-Léger, 8 miles south-east of Arras. Although the Germans were now conducting a different type of battle, with rearguard actions rather than counter-attacks, the fighting was still fierce. Then, on 27 August, the German machine-gun fire began to fade away as the Germans began to withdraw to the relative safety of the Hindenburg Line. For the Guards, success had come at a cost. In six days of fighting, 30 officers and 745 men had been lost.

Captain Thomas Pryce, VC, MC & BAR
GRENADIER GUARDS

Thomas Pryce was born in 1896 in The Hague, the Netherlands. Following school, he attended the Royal Agricultural College, Cirencester, before joining the London Stock Exchange. He later joined the Honourable Artillery Company and was later commissioned into 6th Battalion, The Gloucestershire Regiment before transferring to 4th Battalion Grenadier Guards on 11 September 1916. While serving with The Gloucestershire Regiment he was awarded an MC for conspicuous gallantry at Gommecourt on the night of 25–26 November 1915, followed by a Bar in July 1916.

On 11 April 1918, at Vieux-Berquin in France, Thomas Pryce took part in an action for which he was later awarded the VC. His citation was published in the *London Gazette* on 21 May 1918: 'For most conspicuous bravery, devotion to duty, and self-sacrifice when in command of a flank on the left of the Grenadier Guards. Having been ordered to attack a village he personally led forward two platoons, working from house to house, killing some thirty of the enemy, seven of whom he killed himself. The next day he was occupying a position with some thirty to forty men, the remainder of his company having become casualties. As early as 8.15 a.m., his left flank was surrounded and the enemy was enfilading him. He was attacked no less than four times during the day, and each time beat off the hostile attack, killing many of the enemy. Meanwhile the enemy brought three field guns to within 300 yards of his line, and were firing over open sights and knocking his trench in. At 6.15 p.m., the enemy had worked to within sixty yards of his trench. He then called on his men, telling them to cheer and charge the enemy and fight to the last. Led by Captain Pryce, they left their trench and drove back the enemy with the bayonet some 100 yards. Half an hour later the enemy had again approached in stronger force. By this time Captain Pryce had only 17 men left, and every round of his ammunition had been fired. Determined that there should be no surrender, he once again led his men forward in a bayonet charge, and was last seen engaged in a fierce hand-to-hand struggle with overwhelming numbers of the enemy. With some forty men he had held back at least one enemy battalion for over ten hours. His company undoubtedly stopped the advance through the British line, and thus had great influence on the battle.'

Thomas Pryce was killed in action on 13 April 1918 and has no known grave. His name appears on the Ploegsteert Memorial to the Missing near Ploegsteert, Belgium. His widow, Margaret, was presented with his Victoria Cross at Buckingham Palace by the King, a year later, on 12 April 1918.

The Sixth Regiment of Foot Guards*
THE GUARDS MACHINE GUN REGIMENT

In the early months of the war, infantry battalions were equipped with a machine-gun section of 2 Maxim machine guns, 1 officer and 16 other ranks. But it was not long before there was a greater demand for more and heavier machine guns. In September 1915, just after the formation of the Guards Division, the machine-gun sections from the battalions combined to form three Machine Gun Companies, one for each of the three Guards Brigades. The personnel were drawn from the battalions, and later augmented by machine-gunners trained at schools in England and France, and in February 1917 a Guards Machine Gun Training Centre was formed at Caterham, from where it moved to Epsom at the end of the year. In March 1917, a fourth Guards Machine Gun Company was raised. The companies were granted their own insignia, a five-pointed cap badge, and 'Machine Gun Guards' shoulder patches and brass collar badges, each with two crossed machine guns surmounted by a crown, were worn by their members.

On 10 May 1918, a Royal Warrant was issued, forming the Sixth Regiment of Foot Guards, also known as the Guards Machine Gun Regiment. It was to consist of five battalions: 1st (1st Life Guards) Battalion; 2nd (2nd Life Guards) Battalion; 3rd (Royal Horse Guards) Battalion; 4th (Foot Guards) Battalion (formed from the existing Guards Machine Gun Companies); and 5th (Reserve) Battalion (the Guards Machine Gun Training Centre). The Regiment was equipped with Vickers machine guns.

Opposite: *Guards Machine Gun Corps cap badge.*

Right: *Bugle (with badge).*

As part of this new grouping, the three regiments of Household Cavalry (each less one squadron) were converted into Motor Machine Gun Battalions, (having now finally lost their horses). A new cap badge of the Guards Machine Gun Regiment was approved on 6 November 1918, just a few days before the end of the war.

The tactics for the employment of heavy machine guns evolved quickly, following the general guidelines developed by the Machine Gun Corps. The various types of fire were identified as:

Barrage fire for which up to 60 Vickers machine guns were grouped together just behind the front line firing over the heads of the infantry, out to a range of 1,000 yards and beyond, with the aim of creating a curtain of fire. *Also known as*

Supporting fire in the advance and **covering fire** in the withdrawal.

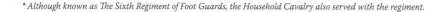

* *Although known as The Sixth Regiment of Foot Guards, the Household Cavalry also served with the regiment.*

Enfilade fire, where the machine guns were aimed at an angle of 45 degrees from the front, one to the left, and the next to the right.

Harassing fire where one or more machine guns concentrated on a specific enemy position, firing in short bursts.

Single-shot fire, when a machine gun was aimed at a single point, for example a sniper or an enemy machine-gun post.

Following the Armistice the days of the Regiment were numbered, although there was hope among some members that it might survive. In February 1919 the three Household Cavalry battalions reverted to their peacetime role. On 22 March 1919 the 4th Battalion took part in the Guards Victory Parade through London, and in June that year provided one guard for the King's Birthday Parade. On 19 July 1919, the Guards Machine Gun Regiment was represented by a detachment on the Victory Parade through London. Recruiting for the Regiment closed in November 1919, and the Regiment was disbanded in February 1920.

THE HINDENBURG LINE

By early September 1918, the Guards Division was back in the area to the west of Cambrai, close to where it had been almost exactly a year earlier, now preparing for one of the last great battles of the war: the crossing of the Canal du Nord and the breaking of the Hindenburg Line. Orders for this operation were issued by Third Army on 19 September while the battalions took the opportunity to become familiar with the ground and the various crossing points along the canal.

Preparations were thorough, as the Royal Engineers gathered together the equipment needed, bridges were constructed, and the various plans and orders promulgated. On the night of 22–23 September, 2nd Guards Brigade, who were to lead the attack in their sector, took over the whole of the Guards Division's frontage of just over 2,000 yards running south-east from the Baupaume–Cambrai road down to the Canal du Nord. The Guards' task in the impending operation was to force their way across the canal, attack the Hindenburg Line beyond, and then advance along the high ground east and north-east of Flesquières.

The battle began on 27 September, with all three Guards brigades involved. In 2nd Guards Brigade, 1st Scots Guards crossed the canal quickly with the help of light ladders to scale the walls. Despite enemy machine-gun fire, the Scots Guards were able to consolidate their positions on the eastern side of the canal.

Below: *The Hindenburg Line and Canal du Nord cutting across the Bapaume–Cambrai road, showing damage from two land mines. The canal was an impressive obstacle. With its construction unfinished, and yet to be filled with water, it was approximately 40 yards wide, with a high bank on the western side.*

Captain Cyril Frisby, VC
COLDSTREAM GUARDS

Cyril Frisby was born in 1885 at Barnet, Hertfordshire. He enlisted as a private in the Royal Hampshire Regiment in 1916, before moving on to the No. 5 Officer Cadet Battalion in December. He was commissioned into the Coldstream Guards in 1917 and was soon serving with 2nd Battalion in France. He was awarded a VC for his actions at the Canal du Nord on 27 September 1918. His citation was published on 27 November 1918: 'For most conspicuous bravery, leadership . . . . across the Canal Du Nord, near Graincourt, when in command of a company detailed to capture the Canal crossing, on the Demicourt–Graincourt road. On reaching the Canal the leading platoon came under annihilating machine-gun fire from a strong machine-gun post under the old iron bridge on the far side of the Canal, and was unable to advance, despite reinforcing waves. Captain Frisby realised at once that unless this post was captured the whole advance in this area would fail. Calling for volunteers to follow him, he dashed forward, and, with three other ranks, he climbed down into the Canal under an intense point-blank machine-gun fire and succeeded in capturing the post with two machine guns and twelve men. By his personal valour and initiative he restored the situation and enabled the attacking companies to continue the advance. Having reached and consolidated his objective, he gave timely support to the company on his right, which had lost all its officers and sergeants, organised its defences, and beat off a heavy hostile counter-attack. He was wounded in the leg by a bayonet in the attack on the machine-gun post, but remained at duty throughout,

thereby setting a splendid example to all ranks.'

Cyril Frisby was presented with his VC by the King at Buckingham Palace on 29 March 1919, retired from the Army in 1920 and joined the London Stock Exchange. He was an excellent sportsman and became a well-known tuna fisherman. He died in 1975 at Guildford, Surrey, and is buried in Brookwood Military Cemetery.

Lance Corporal Thomas Jackson, VC

COLDSTREAM GUARDS

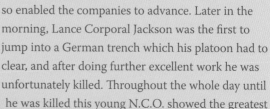

Thomas Jackson was born in 1897 in Swinton, Yorkshire. After leaving school, he was employed by Messrs Ward and Sons, mineral water manufacturers, and later became a cleaner at the Great Central Railway Locomotive Depot at Mexborough, Yorkshire. He enlisted in the Coldstream Guards in 1915, and was later posted to his regiment in France, and promoted to Lance Corporal in June 1918. He was awarded a VC for his actions at the Canal du Nord on 27 September 1918. His citation was published on 27 November 1918: 'For most conspicuous bravery and self-sacrifice in the attack across the Canal Du Nord, near Graincourt. On the morning of the 27 September, 1918, Lance Corporal Jackson was the first to volunteer to follow Capt. C. H. Frisby, Coldstream Guards, across the Canal du Nord in his rush against an enemy machine-gun post. With two comrades he followed his officer across the Canal, rushed the post, captured the two machine-guns, and so enabled the companies to advance. Later in the morning, Lance Corporal Jackson was the first to jump into a German trench which his platoon had to clear, and after doing further excellent work he was unfortunately killed. Throughout the whole day until he was killed this young N.C.O. showed the greatest valour and devotion to duty and set an inspiring example to all'.

Thomas Jackson is buried in Sanders Keep Military Cemetery, Graincourt-les-Havrincourt, France. The cemetery stands on high ground to the east of the canal, and on a clear day the bridge where Cyril Frisby and Thomas Jackson earned their VCs can be clearly seen.

1st Coldstream had a more difficult advance as they came up against two strong German posts at the Demicourt–Graincourt crossing of the canal. It was here that, due to the gallant action and initiative of Captain Cyril Frisby and Lance Corporal Thomas Jackson, the opposition was overcome and the canal crossed. Captain Frisby's company came under heavy fire from the far side of the canal and, with Lance Corporal Jackson and two others, he climbed down into the canal under intense machine-gun fire, and captured the post with 2 machine guns and 12 men. Once on his objective, and having lost all his officers and sergeants, Frisby organised the defence and repelled a heavy counter-attack. He survived the attack, while Jackson was killed and was later buried in a small cemetery that overlooks the bridge where the action took place. They were both awarded the VC for their gallantry that day.

3rd Guards Brigade conducted its crossing with few casualties despite some heavy artillery fire. At around 8.30am, the Brigade HQ crossed, and soon afterwards, the Brigade Commander, Brigadier General Gilbert Follett, was wounded by machine-gun fire and carried

Lieutenant Colonel John Vereker, Viscount Gort,
VC, DSO & TWO BARS, MVO, MC
GRENADIER GUARDS

John Vereker was born in 1886 at East Cowes on the Isle of Wight. He attended the Royal Military College Sandhurst and was commissioned into the Grenadier Guards in August 1905. Most of his service in the pre-war years was with the Grenadier Guards until, in 1913, he became ADC to the GOC London District followed, in 1914, by ADC to General Sir Douglas Haig. On active service with the Grenadiers in France he was awarded an MC and, on 26 September 1917, the Distinguished Service Order, followed by two Bars. The day after, on 27 September, he was to take part in an action for which he was awarded a VC. His citation was published on 27 November 1918: 'For most conspicuous bravery, skilful leading and devotion to duty during the attack of the Guards Division on 27 September, 1918, across the Canal Du Nord, near Flesquières, when in command of the 1st Battalion, Grenadier Guards, the leading battalion of the 3rd Guards Brigade. Under heavy artillery and machine-gun fire he led his battalion with great skill and determination to the "forming-up" ground, where very severe fire from artillery and machine guns was again encountered. Although wounded, he quickly grasped the situation, directed a platoon to proceed down a sunken road to make a flanking attack, and, under terrific fire, went across open ground to obtain the assistance of a tank, which he personally led and directed to

the best possible advantage. While thus fearlessly exposing himself, he was again severely wounded by a shell. Notwithstanding considerable loss of blood, after lying on a stretcher for a while, he insisted on getting up and personally directing the further attack. By his magnificent example of devotion to duty and utter disregard of personal safety all ranks were inspired to exert themselves to the utmost, and the attack resulted in the capture of over 200 prisoners, two batteries of field guns and numerous machine guns. Lt.-Col. Viscount Gort then proceeded to organise the defence of the captured position until he collapsed; even then he refused to leave the field until he had seen the "success signal" go up on the final objective. The successful advance of the battalion was mainly due to the valour, devotion and leadership of this very gallant officer'.

After the war, Lord Gort served on in the Army, becoming Chief of the Imperial General Staff in 1937 and Commander-in-Chief of the British Expeditionary Force in 1939. He commanded throughout the Battle for France, making some of the key decisions that helped save the BEF in June 1940. In 1942 he was appointed Governor and Commander-in-Chief Malta, and promoted to Field Marshal in 1943. He became High Commissioner for Palestine and Trans-Jordan in 1944. He died in Guy's Hospital in London in March 1946 and is buried at Penshurst, Kent.

William Holmes, VC

GRENADIER GUARDS

William Holmes was born in 1895 at Wood Stanway, Gloucestershire. Following school, he worked on the Stanway Estate. He enlisted in The Gloucestershire Regiment in July 1913, transferring to 2nd Grenadier Guards three months later. He served with his regiment during the Retreat from Mons and the First Battle of Ypres. Whilst at the front he suffered from frostbite, had two toes amputated, and spent some time recuperating at home.

He was awarded a VC for his actions on 9 October 1918. His citation was published on 24 December 1918: 'For most conspicuous bravery and devotion to duty at Cattenières on the 9th Oct., 1918. Private Holmes carried in two men under the most intense fire, and, while he was attending to a third case, he was severely wounded. In spite of this, he continued to carry wounded, and was shortly afterwards again wounded, with fatal results.

By his self-sacrifice and disregard of danger he was the means of saving the lives of several of his comrades'. William Holmes was killed on 9 October 1918 and is buried at the Carnières Communal Cemetery Extension, Nord, France. His parents were presented with his VC by King George V on 29 March 1918.

back to a dressing station where he died. Lieutenant Colonel Lord Gort, commanding 1st Grenadiers, was ordered to take over the brigade, and was later awarded a VC for his courage and leadership that day.

The Guards Division was relieved at about 7.30pm on 27 September, a day on which three VCs had been awarded and the Guards had successfully crossed the Canal du Nord and breached the formidable defences along the Hindenburg Line. It had been a remarkable operation, conducted over difficult ground of the enemy's choosing. During the course of the attack the division had captured 25 officers and 703 German soldiers, while its own casualties were 59 officers and 948 men of all ranks.

Left: *A combined infantry and tank advance, 1918.*

Lance Sergeant Harry Wood, VC, MM

SCOTS GUARDS

Harry Wood was born 1882 at Pocklington, North Yorkshire. He joined the Scots Guards in 1902, served with the 2nd Battalion, and was discharged in February 1916 at the end of his service. A year later, in January 1917, he re-joined the Scots Guards, returning to his old battalion. He was awarded a Military Medal for an action on 15 August 1918 when he was surrounded by a group of Germans close to their trench. Taking advantage of his bad luck, he shot two and wounded one who was taken prisoner and later found to be carrying important papers. Two months later, on 13 October 1918 at St Python, France, Wood was involved in an action for which he was awarded the VC. His citation was published on 14 December 1918: 'For most conspicuous bravery and devotion to duty during operations at the village of St. Python, France, on 13 October 1918. The advance was desperately opposed by machine guns and the streets were raked by fire. His platoon sergeant was killed and command of the leading platoon fell to him. The task of the company was to clear the western side of the village and secure the crossing of the River Selle. Command of the ruined bridge had to be gained, though the space in front of it was covered by snipers. Corporal Wood boldly carried a large brick out into the open space, lay down behind it, and fired continually at these snipers, ordering his men to work across while he covered them by his fire. This he continued to do under heavy and well-aimed fire until the whole of his party had reached the objective point. He showed complete disregard for his personal safety, and his leadership throughout the day was of the highest order. Later, he drove off repeated enemy counter-attacks against his position. His gallant conduct and initiative shown, contributed largely to the success of the day's operations'.

Harry Wood was presented with his VC by the King at Buckingham Palace on the 22 February 1919. He was discharged from the Army in July 1919, moving back to York. He later moved to Bristol where he was employed as a commissionaire for the Anglo American Oil Company.

In August 1924, while on holiday in Teignmouth, Wood and his wife were walking along a street when a car mounted the pavement. Mrs Wood managed to push Harry out of the way, only for herself to be pinned against a wall. Mrs Wood recovered from minor cuts and abrasions, but tragically Harry was so shocked by the accident that he fell into a coma from which he never recovered. Harry Wood died aged 42, and is buried in Arnos Vale Cemetery, Bristol.

143

Lieutenent Colonel James Marshall, VC, MC

IRISH GUARDS (ATTACHED 16TH BATTALION LANCASHIRE FUSILIERS)

James Marshall was born in Manchester in 1887. After school, he became a clerk at the Birmingham and Midland Institute and later worked in the Medical Faculty of the University of Birmingham. In 1911, he moved to Harlow where, although not qualified, set himself up as a veterinary surgeon, mainly working with horses. Thereafter, he appeared to spend time abroad, and was serving with a Scottish regiment at the outbreak of war, working in the remount department purchasing horses. He was later commissioned into the Irish Guards, and attached to command the 16th Battalion, Lancashire Fusiliers.

His citation was published in the *London Gazette* on 13 February 1919: 'For most conspicuous bravery, determination and leadership in the attack on the Sambre-Oise Canal, near Catillon, on the 4th November, 1918, when a partly constructed bridge came under concentrated fire and was broken before the advanced troops of his battalion could cross. Lt. Col. Marshall at once went forward and organised parties to repair the bridge. The first party were soon killed or wounded, but by personal example he inspired his command, and volunteers were instantly forthcoming. Under intense fire and with complete disregard of his own safety, he stood on the bank encouraging his men and assisting in the work, and when the bridge was repaired attempted to rush across at the head of his battalion and was killed while so doing. The passage of the canal was of vital importance, and the gallantry displayed by all ranks was largely due to the inspiring example set by Lt. Col. Marshall'.

James Marshall was killed on 4 November 1918, and is buried at Ors Communal Cemetery, close to the village of Ors and between Le Cateau and Landrecies.

MAUBEUGE

On 10 November, Divisional HQ was established in
Maubeuge, and at 7am the following morning, orders
were received regarding the Armistice which was to
come in effect four hours later. When the announcement
came at 11am the news was received 'with no exuberant
outburst of enthusiasm, no wild scenes of rejoicing'. The
statistics of those last few months of the war speak for
themselves. During the 81 days since 21 August and the
Guards Division's first attack in this last phase of the war,
the Guards had spent 54 days in the line, of which 29
had been days of hard fighting. While the Guardsmen
were no doubt relieved that the war was over, they were,
above all, mentally and physically exhausted.

Top: *3rd Grenadier Guards marching into Maubeuge,
10 November 1918.*

Above right: *Men of 1st Irish Guards pass a railway carriage set on
fire by the retreating Germans, near Maubeuge, 10 November 1918.*

Right: *Men of 1st Irish Guards crossing a river using a
wrecked bridge at the village of Assevant, near Maubeuge,
10 November 1918.*

Above: *Irish Guardsmen in a slit trench near Maubeuge, 11 November 1918.*

Above right: *Captain A. W. L. Paget, MC, and Second Lieutenant P. R. J. Barry, MC, of 1st Irish Guards reading news of the Armistice to their men at Maubeuge, 12 November 1918.*

Right: *The mayor of Maubeuge presenting the Maubeuge flag to Major General Torquhil Matheson, GOC Guards Division, March 1919.*

Below right: *The Maubeuge Flag.*

Maubeuge was a pleasant place to spend a few days: fortunately the town had been hardly damaged by the war and the people were immensely friendly. Soon, church services were held, civic receptions took place, and orders were issued for the March to the Rhine which began 18 November.

The Maubeuge Flag, which was specially made in Paris, was presented by the Mayor of Maubeuge to Major General Torquhil Matheson, commanding the Guards Division, in March 1919. The flag was carried on the Guards Victory Parade through London on 22 March 1919, and is now displayed in the Guards Museum at Wellington Barracks.

THE MARCH TO THE RHINE

The weather was cold as the Guards Division set off for their march into Germany where they were to become part of the Army of Occupation. Stephen Graham described the scene in a book published in 1919:

> The road was hard after several days' frost. We are all provided with gloves, which kept our fingers from being chilled, and the march was pleasant . . . . We must have afforded a strange contrast, all rosy cheeked, well-equipped, well-set-up, marching with decision and style, we and the returning British army of prisoners we

Top: *Irish Guards passing Cologne Cathedral, 10 February 1919.*

Right: *A Guardsman in 1918.*

A GUARDSMAN, 1918

met on the road, the haggard-faced soldiers, worn-out and emaciated, who in fives and sixes came struggling from Namur and Charleroi, where they had been liberated in accordance with the Armistice conditions.

On 11 December 1918 the Guards battalions entered Germany and the locals were perhaps friendlier and less hostile than might have been expected after over four years of war. As Graham describes, they 'seemed to be rather afraid of us, and servile, but very poor. Tottering old men insisted on shaking hands with us. The girls of the place seemed to be carefully kept out of our sight.'

By 18 December, the Divisional HQ was established in Cologne and within a few days most of the units had arrived in the city and had been billeted. The distance from Mauberge had been 180 miles although some of the units had actually marched further.

The demobilisation of the Guards Division began soon after Christmas, and by February 1919, 4th Grenadiers, 4th Coldstream and 2nd Irish Guards started to disband in order to keep up the numbers in the remaining battalions.

Above: *Guards ice-hockey match at Cologne, 10 February 1919.*

Below left: *The Grenadier Guards on a route march approaching the Hohenzollern bridge, Cologne, 8 January 1919. A company of 3rd Coldstream, commanded by Captain Lord Falmouth, later experimented with marching in step across this suspension bridge, only to experience the most violent shaking of the roadway.*

At the end of that month, the Guards began their return to England, and on 22 March the Guards Division, led by detachments of the Household Cavalry, marched past King George V at Buckingham Palace, and through London to Mansion House. They were led by Lord Cavan, followed by the Prince of Wales. The two divisional commanders who had followed Lord Cavan led the various brigades, along with brigadiers and other members of staffs. Demobilised officers and soldiers followed on behind their battalions in plain clothes. All Guardsmen who had served during the Great War received on that day a letter signed by King George V in which he thanked them for their service with the Guards Division. He ended the letter with the words 'As your Colonel in Chief I wish to thank you one and all for faithful and devoted Services, and to bid you God-speed, May you ever retain the same mutual feelings of true comradeship which animated and ennobled the life of the Guards Division.'

POST-WAR

Over the next decade, memorials to the Guards,
both along the Western Front and in London were
commissioned and constructed. Most notable among
these was the Guards Memorial which overlooks
Horse Guards from St James's Park. It was designed
by H. Chalton Bradshaw, is built of Portland stone,
and stands 38 feet high. Facing Horse Guards, on a
raised platform, are five bronze statues for each of
the five Regiments of Foot Guards. The statues, by the
sculptor Gilbert Ledward, are slightly larger than life,
and were modelled on Guardsmen serving at the time:
Sergeant Bradshaw, MM, Grenadier Guards; Lance
Corporal Richardson, Coldstream Guards; Guardsman
McDonald, Scots Guards; Guardsman McCarthy,
Irish Guards; and Guardsman Comley, Welsh Guards.
The statues and panels were cast by the Morris Art
Bronze Foundry using bronze from captured guns.

Above: *The Prince of Wales in the Royal Mews, Buckingham Palace, after the Guards Victory Parade, 19 March 1919.*

Left: *The Guards Division Colours in the Victory Parade in Paris, 14 July 1919.*

Below left: *The Grenadier Guards Band and the Colours of the Brigade of Guards passing along Vauxhall Bridge Road during the Victory Parade, London, 19 July 1919.*

Rudyard Kipling provided the inscription:

*To the Glory of God and in the memory of the Officers,
Warrant Officers, Non-Commissioned Officers &
Guardsmen of His Majesty's Regiments of Foot Guards
who gave their lives for their King and Country during
the Great War 1914–1918 and of the Officers, Warrant
Officers, Non-Commissioned Officers and Men of the
Household Cavalry, Royal Regiment of Artillery, Corps
of Royal Engineers, Royal Army Service Corps, Royal
Army Medical Corps and other Units who while serving
the Guards Division in France & Belgium 1915–1918
fell with them in the fight for the World's Freedom.*

The Guards Memorial was unveiled on 16 October 1926 by Field Marshal HRH The Duke of Connaught, assisted by General Sir George Higginson, aged 100. In his article later published in the *Household Brigade Magazine*, Frederick Ponsonby expressed some of the importance and symbolism of the memorial:

Through the length and breadth of our land even the remotest hamlets have raised memorials to those who in the Great War answered the call, left their homes to fight, never to return. Although many of such records bear the names of individual Guardsmen, it is to the historic 'Horse Guards Parade' that our thoughts and steps ever turn, to the one monument to that united brotherhood, unswerving loyalty and indomitable courage which characterized the services of those who left these shores as the Brigade of Guards and later formed the unique and unconquerable Guards Division. Here, for all time, stands the emblem of loving memory and undying honours to all who on the battlefields of France and Flanders testified theirs was that love than which none is greater.

Left: *The Household Cavalry Memorial at Zandvoorde, unveiled by Field Marshal Earl Haig on 4 May 1924, commemorates the 120 members of 1st Life Guards, 159 members of 2nd Life Guards, and the 62 members of The Royal Horse Guards (The Blues) who died in France and Flanders in 1914. The inscription on the memorial reads:*

*To Those
of The 1st & 2nd Life Guards & Royal Horse Guards
who died fighting in France & Flanders, 1914
Many of them fell in defence of the ridge
upon which this cross stands*

Above and right: *The unveiling of the Guards Memorial in 1926; the Guards Memorial today, bearing bomb damage from the Second World War.*

Opposite left: *Chaplains at the unveiling of the Guards Memorial. Left to right: Rev. A. R. Yeoman, Chaplain General, Scottish Command; Rev. W. B. Hughes, Guards Chapel, Wellington Barracks; Rev. O. S. Watkin, Deputy Chaplain General; Rev. Guy Standing, Western Command, Chester; Rev. Father B. McGuinness, R. C. Chaplain, Aldershot.*

Below: *Guillemont Road Cemetery, Somme, France, one of many cemeteries where soldiers of the Guards regiments are buried.*

'The Soul Of the Guards'

GENERAL LORD RAWLINSON

For many years, indeed for some centuries, it has been the proud prerogative of Guardsmen to acquire and to maintain the highest form of military discipline, a discipline which, whilst demanding the meticulous obedience of the spirit as well as the letter of every order, is founded upon confidence: in superiors and respect of authority, rather than upon the fear of punishment.

Whilst, on the other hand, the NCOs and men are thoroughly imbued with the paramount necessity for subordinating their individual inclinations to the will of their officers, these officers are correspondingly taught not to abuse that authority, but to win the confidence of those whom they command, by a high personal example, by their devotion to the welfare of their men and by thorough efficiency in all their military duties.

Nothing is more vital to the success of any leader of men than the possession of the confidence of those he commands. He cannot win that confidence except he be in himself a thorough and efficient soldier who knows his business in every detail. Nor is this sufficient, for, in addition, he must possess the characteristics of an officer and a gentleman, constantly devoting his undivided attention to the instruction, the welfare and, I would add, the recreations of those under his immediate command.

Though during the first half of the last century discipline meant less than it does today, the historic deeds of the Guards in the Peninsular, at Waterloo, and in the Crimea, were the direct outcome of discipline and sound leadership. Based on that tradition, and fostered under the sense of example to the rest of the Army, our Guards Battalions more than maintained their high reputation in Egypt in the 'eighties and in South Africa at the beginning of the present century. At Belmont, at Modder River, and on many subsequent occasions, Guards Battalions added lustre to the great traditions of Inkerman, the Alma, and Tel-el-Kebir.

It has been precisely the same story in the Great War in France.

No higher compliment could be paid to the Guards' system than the fact that, as the Great War dragged on, other Divisions, including some from the Dominions, made it their business to adopt the methods which have always prevailed in the Brigade of Guards. The Drill Instructors and senior NCOs of the Guards Division were in constant demand throughout the Army in France, a demand which could not, of course, be wholly met. But the point I desire to make clear is that the Guards' system when put to the severest possible test on the blood-stained battlefields of France, came through triumphant and was by acclamation recognised as a paramount factor in the great ordeal of battle.

It was the Guards Battalions which best withstood the supreme test of endurance demanded of them in the Retreat from Mons, and at Ypres, in 1914. At Loos, when the Guards Division first went into action as a Division, they greatly distinguished themselves under particularly trying circumstances amongst surroundings where a less staunch and determined attitude might easily have caused disaster. Many other instances of

the inestimable value of discipline could be found; notably in the most costly of all individual engagements, September 15th 1916, at Ginchy during the Somme battle, where, as I told them at the time, they won the honours of the day by their gallantry and valour; and again in November, 1917, when the German counter-attack at Gouzeaucourt, near Cambrai, was checked and held by the steadiness and local initiative of the Guards Division.

It is not my purpose nor is there need to examine the details of our system, which are well known to all Guardsmen, and which have been handed down to us by past generations. But in the face of certain criticisms that have been made by people who know no better,

Above: *VC winners of the Brigade of Guards with Lord Gort. Front row, left to right: George Henry Wyatt, Oliver Brooks, John Vaughan Campbell, Viscount Gort, Robert Bye, Fred McNess. Back row, left to right: John Moyney, George Boyd-Rochfort, Cyril Frisby, Wilfred Fuller, John McCaulay, George Evans.*

I repeat that in its essence is the confidence, the trust, and the good comradeship between officers and men, founded on the one hand on the implicit obedience of the subordinate, and, on the other, on the tactful but rigid employment of unquestioned authority by those in command.

It is this which makes us all proud to be Guardsmen.

Household Brigade Magazine, Victory Edition, 1920

BIBLIOGRAPHY

Anglesey, The Marquess of, *A History Of The British Cavalry 1816–1919, Volume 7: The Curragh Incident And The Western Front, 1914* (Barnsley: Pen & Sword, 1994)

Arthur, Captain Sir George, *The Story of the Household Cavalry, Volume III* (London: William Heinemann, 1926)

Ball, Simon, *The Guardsmen: Harold Macmillan, Three Friends, and the World They Made* (London: HarperCollins, 2004)

Batchelor, Peter and Christopher Matson, *VCs of the First World War: The Western Front 1915* (Stroud: The History Press, 2011)

Blades, Geoffrey, *The Forgotten Battle, Hazebrouck 1918* (Geoffrey Blades, 1991, 1992)

Bond, Brian, *Survivors of a Kind: Memoirs of the Western Front* (London: Continuum, 2008)

Briant, Keith, *Fighting with the Guards* (London: Evans Brothers, 1958)

Carstairs, Carroll, *A Generation Missing* (London: William Heinemann, 1930)

Craster, Michael, *'Fifteen Rounds a Minute': The Grenadiers at War, August to December 1914, Edited from the Diaries and Letters of Major 'Ma' Jeffreys and Others* (Barnsley: Pen & Sword, 1976)

Colville, J. R., *Man of Valour: Field-Marshal Lord Gort V.C.* (London: Collins, 1972)

Ewart, Wilfrid, *Scots Guard: On the Western Front, 1915–1918* (1934)

Fryer E. R. M., *Grenadier: The Recollections of an Officer of the Grenadier Guards throughout the Great War on the Western Front* (Driffield: Leonaur, 2009).

Gibbs, Gary, *The Brigade of Guards: Victoria and George Cross Winners* (London: The Guards Museum, 2012)

Gilbert, Martin, *Winston S. Churchill, Volume III: The Challenge of War, 1914–1916* (London: Heinemann, 1971)

Gliddon, Gerald, *VCs of the First World War: Somme 1916* (Stroud: The History Press, 2012)

Goodinge, Anthony, *The Scots Guards* (London: Leo Cooper, 1969)

Headlam, Cuthbert, *History of the Guards Division in The Great War 1915–1918* (London: John Murray, 1924)

Holmes, Richard, *Riding the Retreat: Mons to the Marne 1914 Revisited* (London: Jonathan Cape, 1995)

Horne, Alistair, *Harold Macmillan Volume I: 1894–1956* (London: Macmillan, 1988)

Household Brigade Magazine and its successor, *The Guards Magazine*

Irish Guards: The First Hundred Years, 1900–2000 (Staplehurst: Spellmount, 2000)

Jones, Spencer, "The Demon': Brigadier-General Charles FitzClarence V.C.' in Spencer Jones (ed.), *Stemming the Tide: Officers and Leadership in the British Expeditionary Force 1914*, pp.240–262 (Solihull: Helion & Company, 2013)

Kipling, Rudyard, *The Irish Guards in the Great War: The Second Battalion* (Staplehurst: Spellmount, 1997)

Lambart, Lady Nell, *FM The Earl of Cavan: A Life.* [Published privately.]

Leask, Anthony, *Putty, From Tel-el-Kebir to Cambrai: The Life and Letters of Lieutenant General Sir William Pulteney 1861–1941* (Solihull: Helion & Company, 2015)

Liddell Hart, B. H., *History of the First World War* (London: Cassell, 1970)

Lindsay, Donald, *Forgotten General: A Life of Andrew Thorne* (Salisbury: Michael Russell, 1987)

Lloyd, R. A., *A Trooper in the 'Tins': Autobiography of a Lifeguardsman* (London: Hurst & Blackett, 1938)

Lyttelton, Oliver, Viscount Chandos, *The Memoirs of Lord Chandos* (London: The Bodley Head, 1962)

Masefield, John, *The Old Front Line* (Barnsley: Pen & Sword, 2003)

Morris, Richard, *The Man Who Ran London During the Great War: The Diaries and Letters of Lieutenant General Sir Francis Lloyd, GCVO, KCB, DSO, 1853–1926* (Barnsley, Pen & Sword, 2009)

Nicolson, Nigel, *Alex: The Life of Field Marshal Earl Alexander of Tunis* (London: Weidenfeld & Nicolson, 1973)

Paget, Julian, *Second To None: The History of the Coldstream Guards, 1650–2000* (Barnsley, Pen & Sword, 2001)

A post-war letter from The Prince of Wales: 'I am very glad to hear that the Household Brigade Magazine is to come out again.'

Paget, Julian, *The Story of the Guards* (London: Osprey Publishing, 1976)

Petre, F. Loraine, Wilfrid Ewart and Major-General Sir Cecil Lowther, *The Scots Guards in The Great War, 1914–18* (Uckfield: Naval & Military Press, 2002)

Retallack, John, *The Welsh Guards* (London: Frederick Warne, 1981)

Ross-of-Bladensburg, Lieutenant Colonel Sir John, *The Coldstream Guards, 1914–1918*, Volumes I & II (London: Oxford University Press, 1928)

Royle, Trevor, *Bearskins, Bayonets & Body Armour: Welsh Guards 1915–2015* (Barnsley: Frontline Books, 2015)

Sitwell, Osbert, *Great Morning* (London: Macmillan, 1948)

Soames, Mary (ed.), *Speaking for Themselves: The Personal Letters of Winston and Clementine Churchill* (London: Doubleday, 1998)

Sparham, Anna (with contributions by Margaret Denny, Diane Atkinson and Hilary Roberts), *Soldiers & Suffragettes: The Photography of Christina Broom* (London: Philip Wilson Publishers/The Museum of London, 2015)

Stourton, Harry, *FM The Earl of Cavan: His Campaign in Italy, 1917–1919*

Terraine, John, *Mons: The Retreat to Victory* (London: B. T. Batsford, 1960)

Verney, Peter, *The Micks: The Story of the Irish Guards* (London: Macmillan, 1973)

White-Spunner, Barney, *Horse Guards* (London: Macmillan, 2006)

Whitworth, R. H., *The Grenadier Guards* (London: Leo Cooper, 1974)

William II [former German Emperor], *My Early Life* (London: Methuen & Co, 1926)

Wright, Philip, *For Distinguished Conduct* (Blurb, 2012)

Wyndham, Captain The Honourable Reginald, The First World War Diary of Captain Hon W. R. Wyndham LG. 5 October– 4 November 1914. [Private papers.]

Ziegler, Philip, *King Edward VIII: The Official Biography* (London: Collins, 1990)

ST JAMES'S PALACE. S.W.

I am very glad to hear that the Household Brigade Magazine is to come out again, and I wish it the same success in the future as it enjoyed before the war.

Edward P

March 11th, 1920.

INDEX

Picture credits

Every effort has been made to contact the copyright holders of
all images featured in this book. In the case of an inadvertent
omission, please contact the publisher.

The publisher would like to thank the following agencies, institutions
and individuals for permission to use their material. Special thanks
are extended to the staff at the IWM for their assistance.

125b The Art Archive/Imperial War Museum; 107 Sean Bolan;
69 Cazalet family archive; 45b, 97t © Chronicle/Alamy Stock
Photo; 48t Coldstream Guards Archives; 91 © Corbis; 38r Simon
Doughty; 7 The Grenadier Guards; 38l, 81, 103, 128 Grenadier
Guards Archives; back cover, 2–3, 41b, 74, 74–75, 106r, 113r,
136–137, 137, 146bl The Guards Museum, London/George
Ramsay; 99 Frank Haslam; 14–15, 79, 109, 150l, 155t *Household
Brigade Magazine*; 20b, 25 both, 55, 115r Household Cavalry
Museum; 116 Officers' Mess, Household Cavalry Regiment,
Combermere Barracks, Windsor; 28 Officers' Mess, Household
Cavalry Mounted Regiment, Hyde Park Barracks; 117l, 146tr
Hulton Archive/Stringer/Getty; 23, 36, 92, 106l © Illustrated
London News Ltd/Mary Evans; 41t, 89 by kind permission of the
Irish Guards; front cover, 16t, 19b, 24, 29r, 40, 42, 43, 44, 47l, 47r,
54b, 56, 57, 60–61, 62b, 63, 64, 65t, 68, 72 all, 73, 76br, 82, 83l,
84–85, 93t, 94–95, 97b, 100, 104, 105, 110–111, 113l, 114, 115l,
117r, 119, 120, 121 both, 123, 124 both, 126, 127r, 130t, 132–133,
138, 139, 140, 142t, 142b, 144, 145 all, 146tl, 146br, 147t, 148

both, 149 all, 150–151, 151bl, 153 © IWM; 87 Jaron James © de
László Foundation; 12, 22, 147b from Headlam, Cuthbert, *History
of the Guards Division in The Great War 1915–1918* (London:
John Murray, 1924); 29l, 67t © Look and Learn; 17 from Sitwell,
Osbert, *Great Morning* (Macmillan, 1948); 21b Mary Evans
Picture Library/Charlotte Zeepvat; 51, 52 from Lindsay, Donald,
Forgotten General: A Life of Andrew Thorne (Salisbury: Michael
Russell, 1987); 4, 19t, 20tl, 21t, 26–27 © Museum of London/
Christina Broom Collection; 30–31, 34–35, 49 Courtesy of the
Council of the National Army Museum, London; 20tr, 76bl,
76t, 93b, 102, 127l, 129, 141, 155b © National Portrait Gallery,
London; 53 © Pictorial Press Ltd/Alamy Stock Photo; 80, 125t
Popperfoto/Getty; 45t Private Collection/Bridgeman Images; 70
Private Collection/© Look and Learn/Elgar Collection/Bridgeman
Images; 77 Private Collection/The Stapleton Collection/
Bridgeman Images; 32 © Royal Hospital Chelsea, London, UK/
Bridgeman Images; 151bl © Maurice Savage/Alamy Stock
Photo; 88b © Seapix/Alamy Stock Photo; 98 Scots Guards
Archives; 96 © Peter Stone Archive/Alamy Stock Photo; 118 ©
Towneley Hall Art Gallery and Museum, Burnley, Lancashire/
Bridgeman Images; 88t Universal History Archive/Getty; 67b IF
SL 00-838: "Sergeant Mike O'Leary, V. C.," 1915, Francis, Day &
Hunter: London. Image courtesy of: Ward Irish Music Archives,
Milwaukee Irish Fest Collection, accession 1998.002; 9, 151r Matt
Wilson; 33, 37, 128, 135 www.ww1photos.com; 58 Wyndham
family archive; 59 Samantha Wyndham